Math in FOCUS®

Singapore Math®
by Marshall Cavendish

1A

Workbook

Consultant and Author
Dr. Fong Ho Kheong

Authors
Chelvi Ramakrishnan and Bernice Lau Pui Wah

U.S. Consultants
Dr. Richard Bisk, Andy Clark, and Patsy F. Kanter

mc Marshall Cavendish
Education

U.S. Distributor

Houghton
Mifflin
Harcourt

© 2015 Marshall Cavendish Education Private Limited

Published by Marshall Cavendish Education
An imprint of Marshall Cavendish Education Private Limited
Times Centre, 1 New Industrial Road, Singapore 536196
Customer Service Hotline: (65) 6213 9444
U.S. Office Tel: (1-914) 332 8888 Fax: (1-914) 332 8882
E-mail: tmesales@mceducation.com
Website: www.mceducation.com

Distributed by
Houghton Mifflin Harcourt
222 Berkeley Street
Boston, MA 02116
Tel: 617-351-5000
Website: www.hmheducation.com/mathinfocus

First published 2015

Math in Focus® Workbook 1A
ISBN 978-0-544-19380-2

Printed in Singapore

1 2 3 4 5 6 7 8   1401   20 19 18 17 16 15
4500463701   A B C D E

Contents

Addition Facts to 10

Subtraction Facts to 10

CHAPTER 5

Shapes and Patterns

CHAPTER 6

Ordinal Numbers and Position

CHAPTER 7 Numbers to 20

CHAPTER 8 Addition and Subtraction Facts to 20

CHAPTER 9 Length

CHAPTER 1 Numbers to 10

Practice 1   Counting to 10

Count.
Write the numbers.

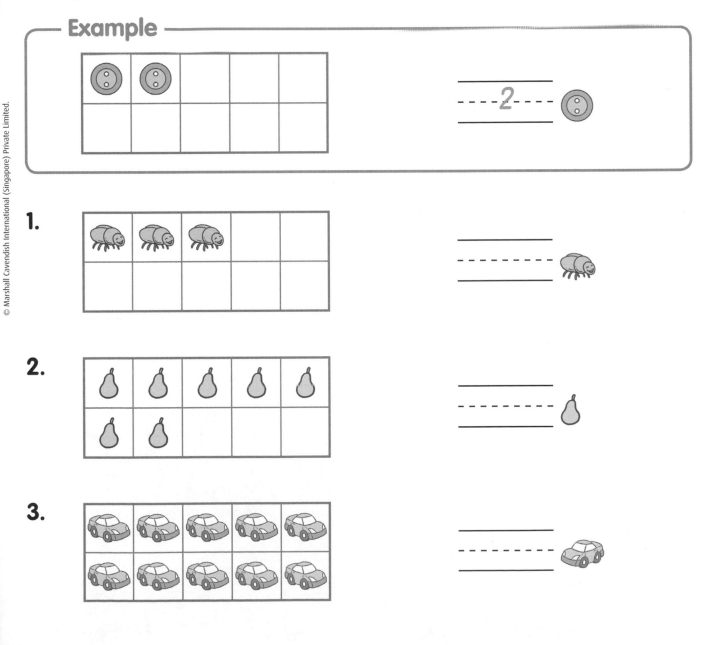

Example

2

1.

_____

2.

_____

3.

_____

Count.
Write the numbers.

4.

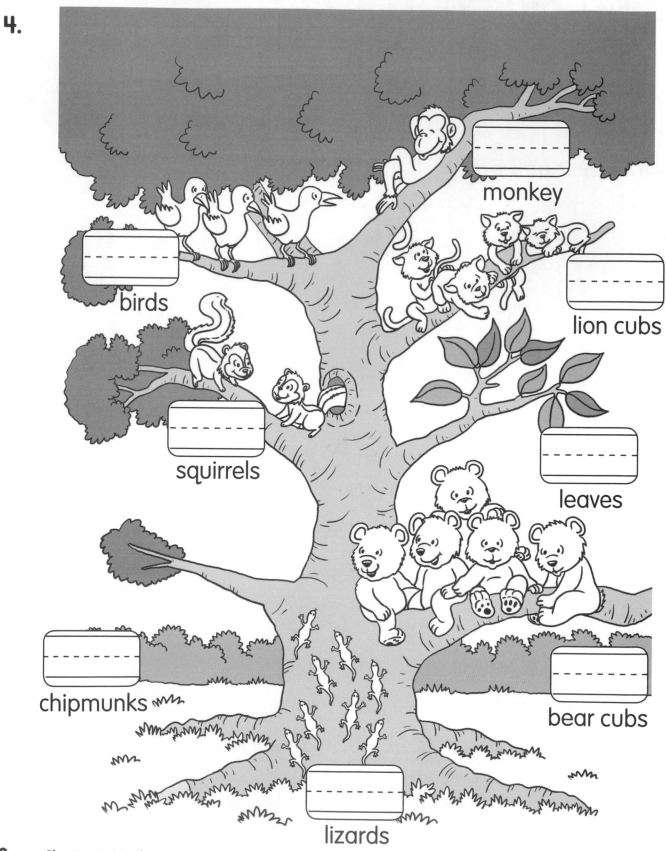

monkey

birds

lion cubs

squirrels

leaves

chipmunks

bear cubs

lizards

Name: _____   Date: _____

Draw.

5.   A cow has 2 horns.

6.   A chair has 4 legs.

7.   An ant has 6 legs.

8.   Each ladybug has 10 spots.

How many insects are there?
Match.

9.

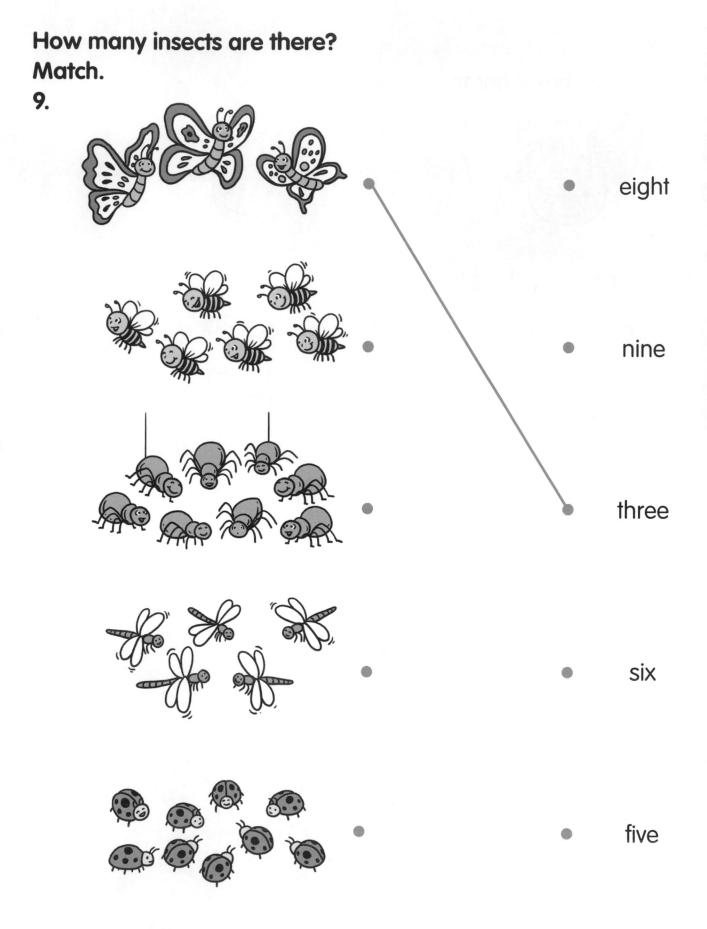

eight

nine

three

six

five

Name: _____   Date: _____

Count the things on the snowman.
Circle the correct words.

10.		two	three	four	five	zero
11.		zero	one	two	three	four
12.		six	seven	eight	nine	ten
13.		one	two	three	four	five
14.		nine	six	one	eight	three

Match the numbers to the words.

15.

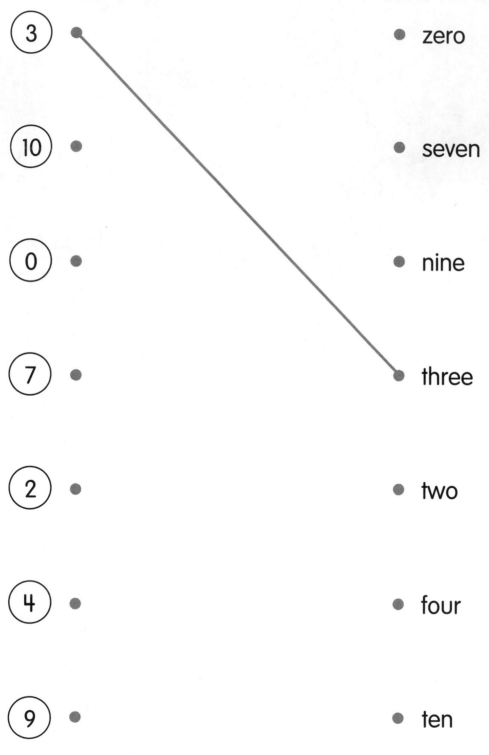

Practice 2   Comparing Numbers

Count.
Circle the groups that have the same number.

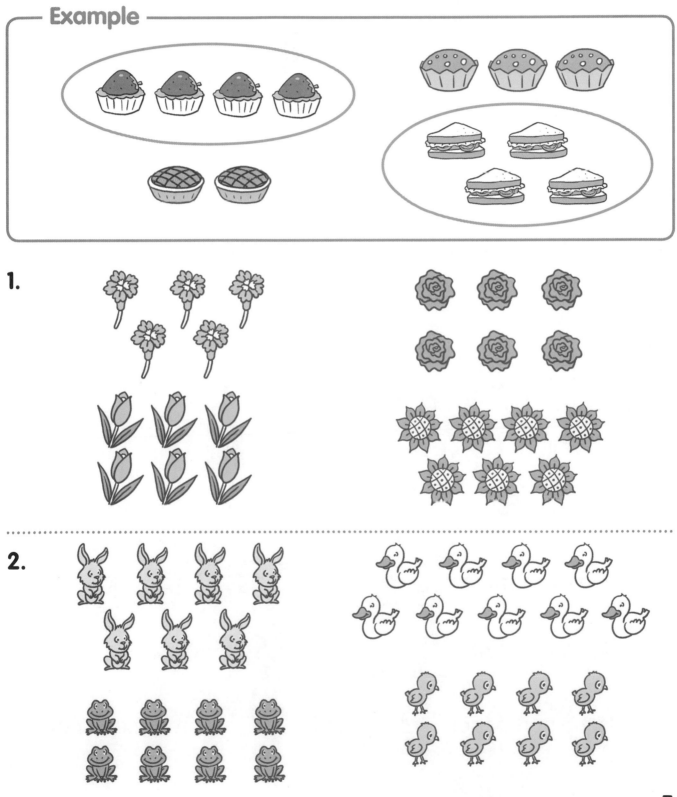

Match. Then circle the answer to each question.

Example

Are there more than ? (Yes) No

Are there fewer than ? Yes (No)

Is the number of and the same? Yes (No)

3.

Are there more than ? Yes   No

Are there fewer than ? Yes   No

Is the number of and the same?   Yes   No

Match. Then circle the answer.

4.

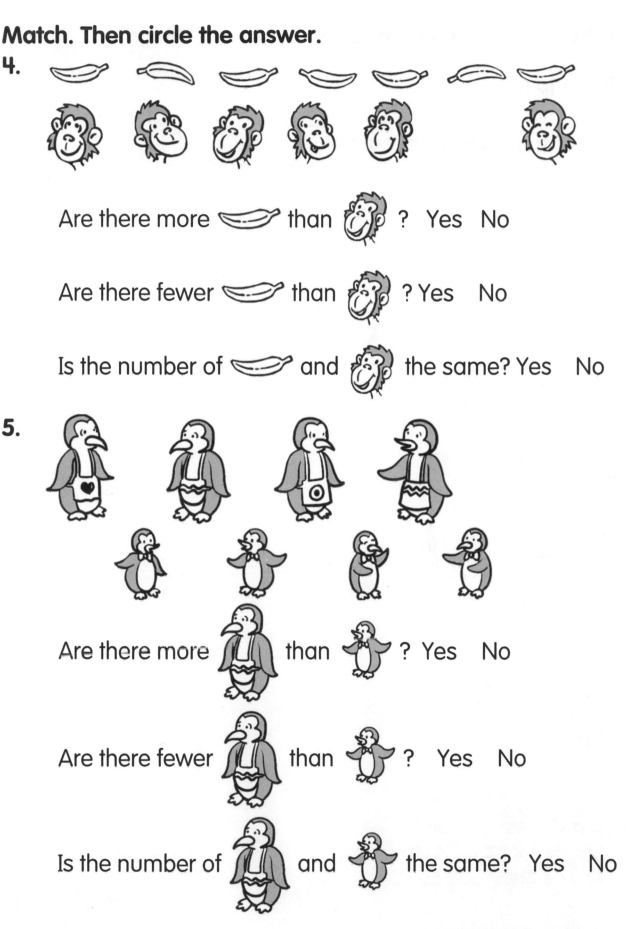

Are there more 🍌 than 🐵 ? Yes No

Are there fewer 🍌 than 🐵 ? Yes No

Is the number of 🍌 and 🐵 the same? Yes No

5.

Are there more 🐧 than 🐧 ? Yes No

Are there fewer 🐧 than 🐧 ? Yes No

Is the number of 🐧 and 🐧 the same? Yes No

Which two groups have the same number of things?

Join them to a ------ .

Then write the number in each ------ .

6.

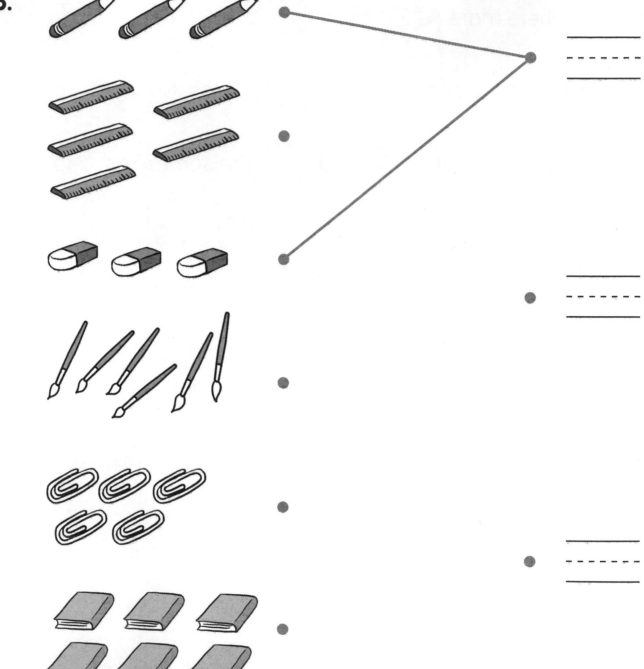

Name: _____   Date: _____

Count and write the number.
Then answer each question by coloring the correct box.

Which is more?

┌─ **Example** ───┐
│   │
│   ___4___ [pots 🍲]   ___6___ [pears 🍐]   │
│   │
└──┘

7.   _____ [cups ☕]   _____ [teapot 🫖]

Which is fewer?

8.   _____ [ladles 🥄]   _____ [muffins 🧁]

9.   _____ [gloves 🧤]   _____ [plates 🍽]

Color the correct signs.

Which number is greater?

10.   5   8

11.   10   9

Which number is less?

12.   7   3

13.   1   6

Write the numbers in the blanks.

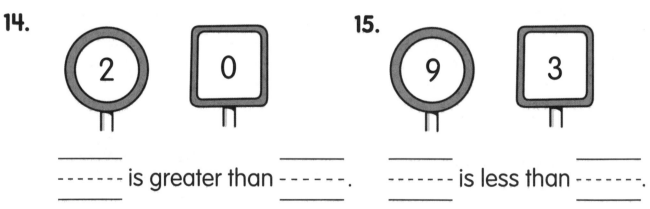

14.   2   0

_____ is greater than _____.

15.   9   3

_____ is less than _____.

Color the flags with the same number.

16.

8   6   9   6

Practice 3 Making Number Patterns

What comes next in each pattern?
Write the number.

1.

_____

2.

_____

3.

_____

What is 1 more?
Write the number.

4.

_____

5.

_____

6.

_____

What is 1 less?
Write the number.

7.

8.

9.

Write the missing numbers in the number patterns.

10.

| 4 | 5 | | | 8 |

11.

| 0 | 1 | | | 4 |

Name: _____ **Date:** _____

Write the missing numbers in the number patterns.

12.

13.

14.

15.

Fill in the blanks.

16. 1 more than 1 is _____ .

17. 1 more than 8 is _____ .

18. 1 more than 9 is _____ .

19. 1 less than 7 is _____ .

20. 1 less than 9 is _____ .

21. 1 less than 6 is _____ .

22. _____ is 1 more than 3.

23. _____ is 1 more than 6.

24. _____ is 1 less than 4.

25. _____ is 1 less than 7.

Put On Your Thinking Cap!

Challenging Practice

Mother Hen's eggs have numbers that are greater than 2 and less than 8.

Color the eggs that belong to Mother Hen.

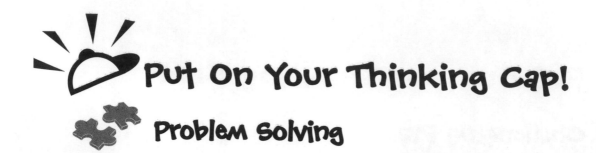

Put On Your Thinking Cap!

Problem Solving

Daryl sees a pattern made with △.

He wants to continue the pattern but does not know
how many △ to draw.

**Draw the next group of △ in the box below to continue
the pattern.**

There are _____ △ in the next group.

Name: _____   Date: _____

Chapter Review/Test

Vocabulary

Match.

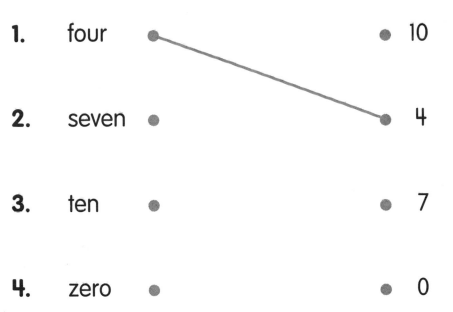

1. four

2. seven

3. ten

4. zero

   10

   4

   7

   0

Concepts and Skills

Circle the stars to show the number.
Write the number in words.

5. 5

_____

6. 9

_____

Fill in the blanks with *greater than, less than or the same as*.

cups and saucers   trees   cars

7.   The number of cups is _____ the number
      of saucers.

8.   The number of trees is _____ the number of cars.

9.   The number of cars is _____ the number of cups.

Write any two numbers.

10.   greater than 5: _____ _____.

11.   less than 7: _____ _____.

Write the missing numbers in the number pattern.

12.

(6) (5) (4) (   ) (   ) (1) (   )

Fill in the blanks.

13.   4 is 1 less than _____.

14.   9 is 1 more than _____.

Name: _____   Date: _____

CHAPTER 2 Number Bonds

Practice 1   Making Number Bonds

Look at the ▨.
Fill in the parts.

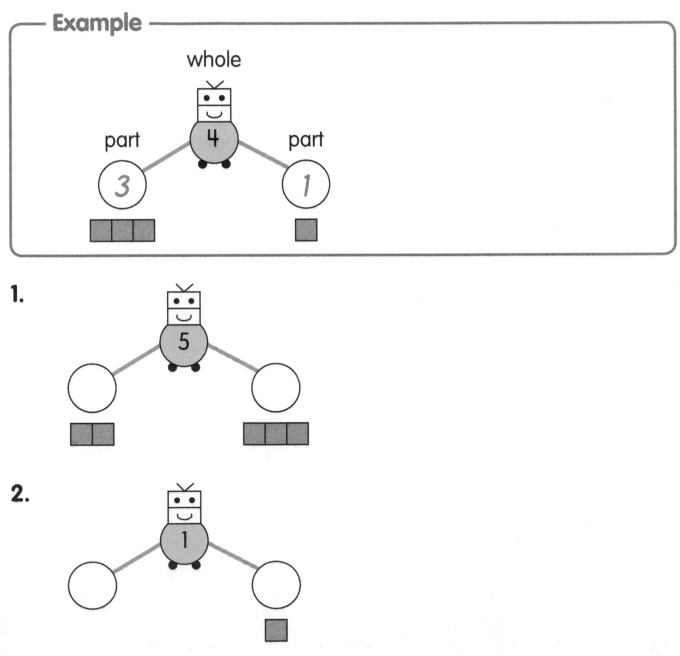

Look at the ▨.
Fill in the whole.

Example

part   part

whole

3.

4   1

4.

0   3

5.

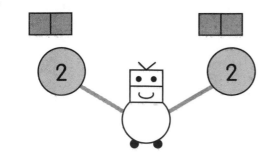

2   2

Look at the ▮.
Fill in the parts.

┌─ **Example** ──────────────────────────────────────┐

└──┘

6.

7.

8.

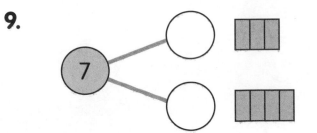

9.

Complete the number bonds.
Fill in the blanks.

10. What numbers make 10?

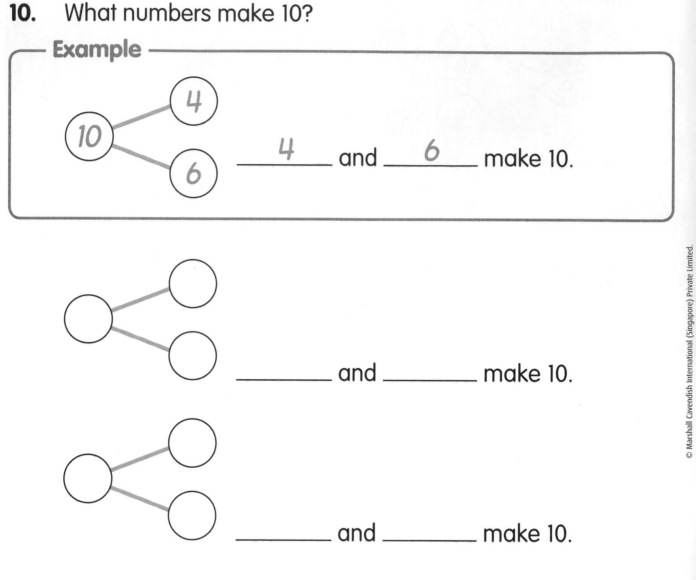

Example

_____4_____ and _____6_____ make 10.

_____ and _____ make 10.

_____ and _____ make 10.

11. Are there any other numbers that make 10?

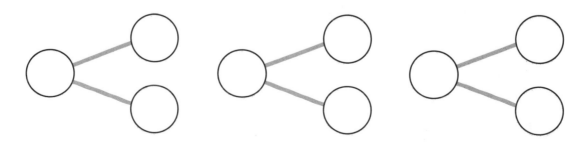

Practice 2 Making Number Bonds

Look at the pictures.
Complete the number bonds.

Example

1.

2.

Look at the pictures.
Complete the number bonds.

3.

4.

5.

6.

Practice 3 Making Number Bonds

Match to make 8.

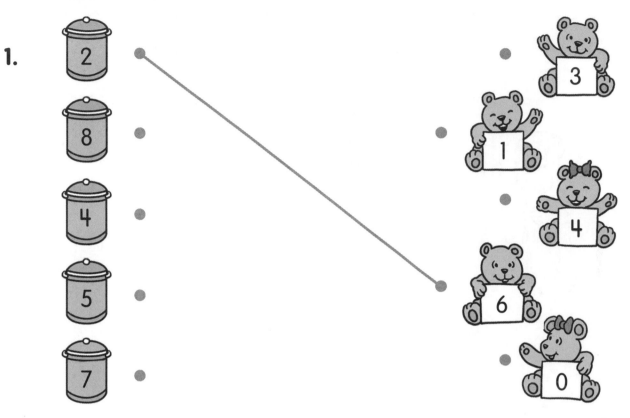

1.

Match the numbers.

2. Match to make 6.

3. Match to make 9.

Look at the picture.
Complete the number bonds.

4.

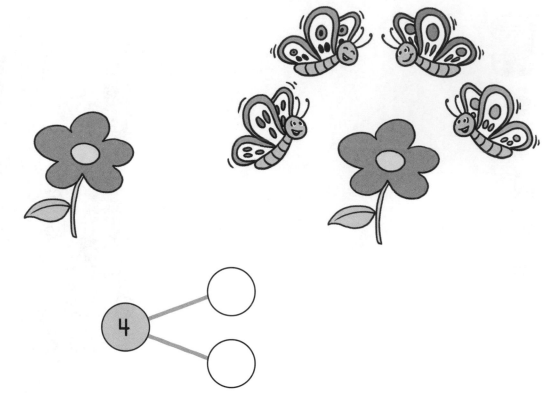

Look at the number bond.
Draw the correct number of butterflies.

5.

Name: _____ Date: _____

Use two colors. Color the ☐ to show two numbers
that make the number in ⬭.
Complete the number bonds.
Fill in the blanks.

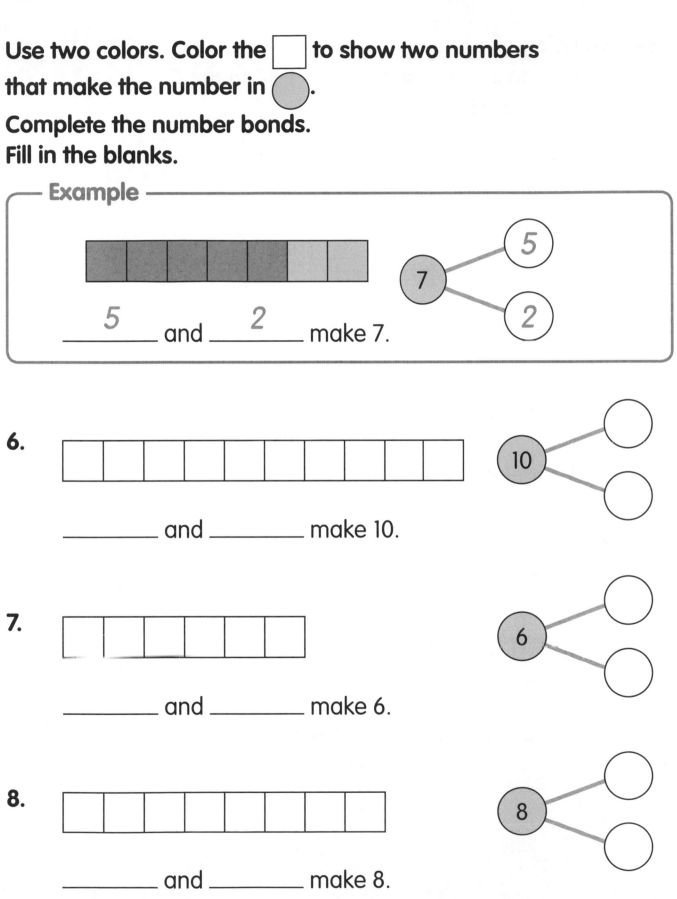

Example

_____5_____ and _____2_____ make 7.

6.

_____ and _____ make 10.

7.

_____ and _____ make 6.

8.

_____ and _____ make 8.

Use two colors.
Color the ☐ to show two numbers that make 5.
Complete the number bonds.
Fill in the blanks.

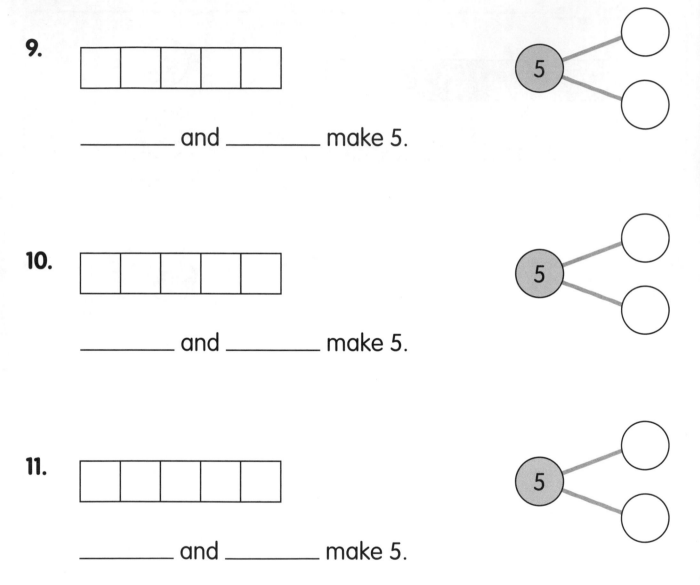

9.

_____ and _____ make 5.

10.

_____ and _____ make 5.

11.

_____ and _____ make 5.

Put On Your Thinking Cap!

Challenging Practice

Make a number bond with three numbers from the bag.
Use each number once.

1.

2.

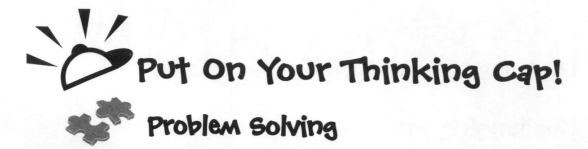

Put On Your Thinking Cap!

Problem Solving

Write five numbers from 1 to 10 on each clown
to complete the number bonds.
Use each number once for each clown.

Example

8

3   5

2   1   4

1.

10

2.

9

Chapter Review/Test

Vocabulary
Choose the correct word.

1.

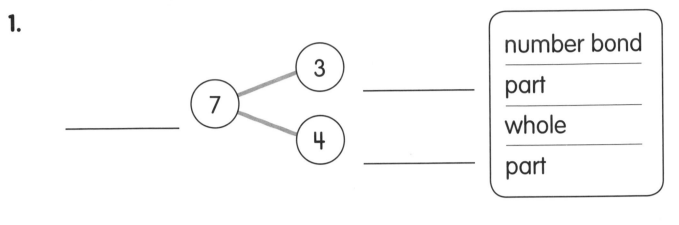

number bond
part
whole
part

2.   3, 4, and 7 make a _____.

Concepts and Skills
Complete the number bonds.
Fill in the blanks.

3.

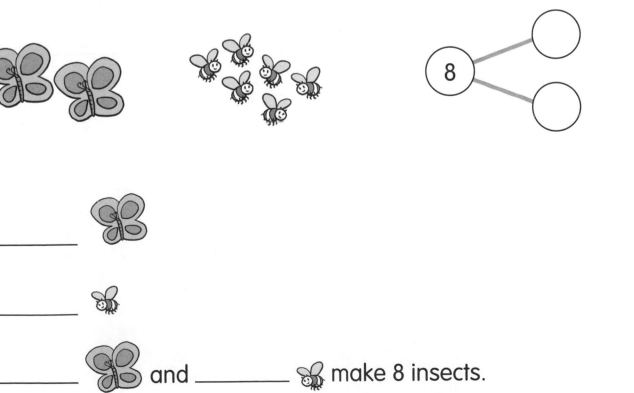

_____ 🦋

_____ 🐝

_____ 🦋 and _____ 🐝 make 8 insects.

What numbers make 7?

4.

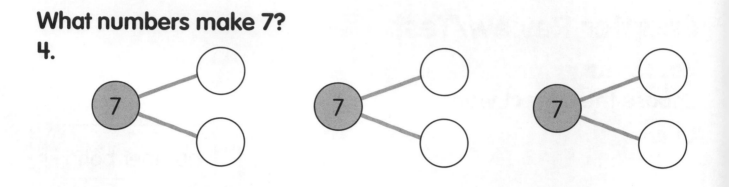

Look at the picture.
Complete the number bond.
Fill in the blanks.

5.

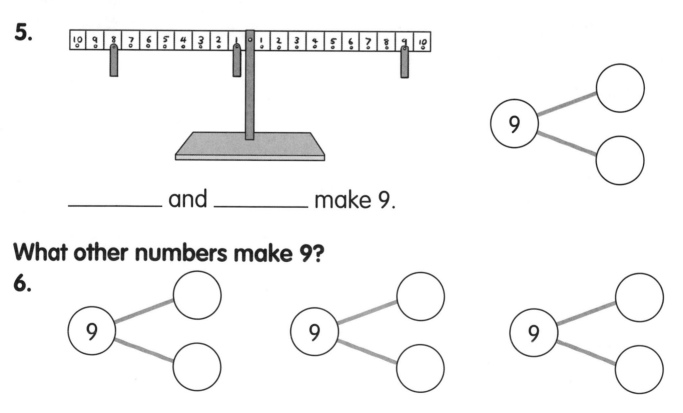

_____ and _____ make 9.

What other numbers make 9?

6.

Cumulative Review

for Chapters 1 and 2

Concepts and Skills

Count.
Write the numbers.

1.

There are _____ 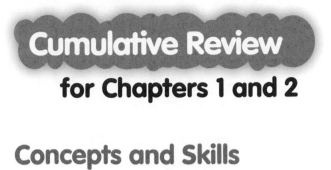 .

2.

There are _____ .

3.

There are _____ .

Match the numbers to the words.

4.

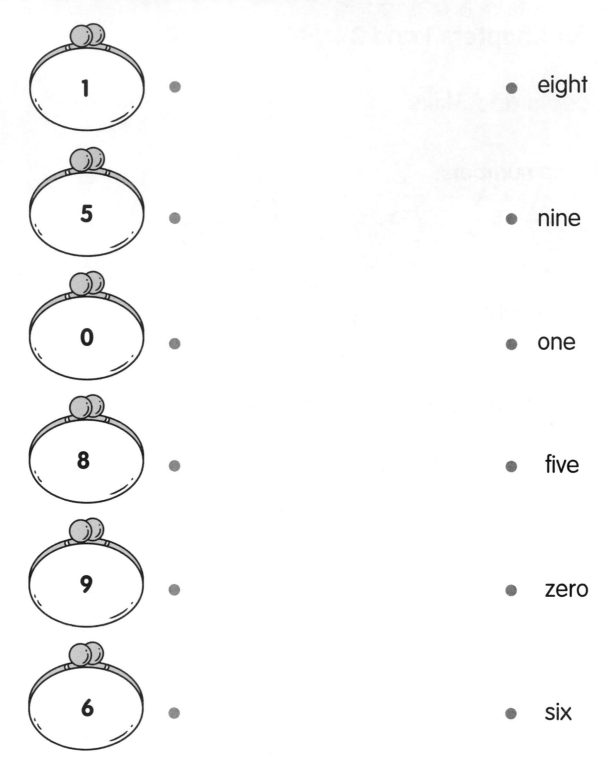

1 • • eight

5 • • nine

0 • • one

8 • • five

9 • • zero

6 • • six

Circle the group that has <u>more</u>.

5.

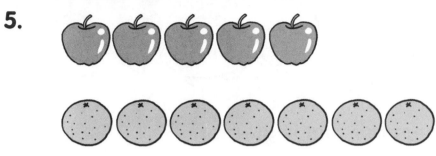

Circle the group that has <u>fewer</u>.

6.

Circle the groups that have the <u>same</u> number.

7.

Color the fish with the number that is <u>less</u>.

8.

9.

Color the fish with the number that is <u>greater</u>.

10.

11.

Complete the number patterns.

12.

13.

Fill in the blanks.

14. 1 more than 5 is _____.

15. _____ is 1 less than 7.

Name: _____   **Date:** _____

Count and complete each number bond.
Then fill in the blanks.

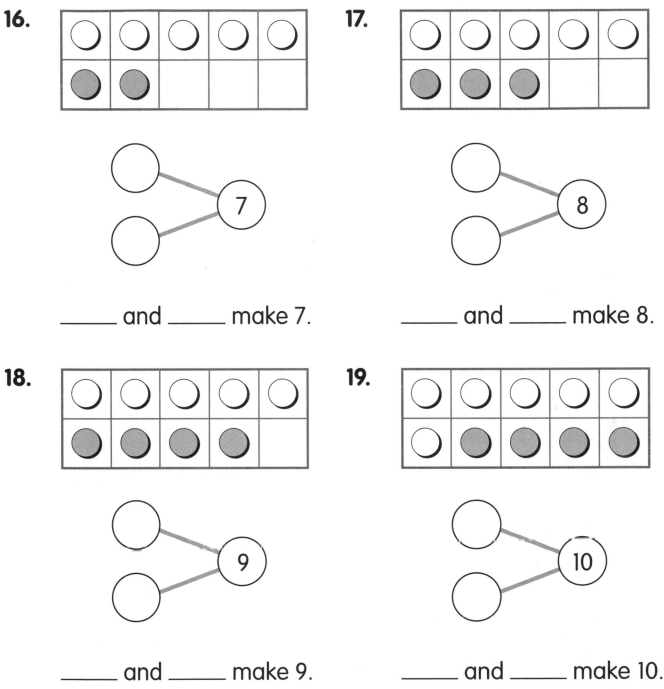

16.

_____ and _____ make 7.

17.

_____ and _____ make 8.

18.

_____ and _____ make 9.

19.

_____ and _____ make 10.

Write the missing numbers.
 stands for a number.

20.

 is _____.

21.

 is _____.

22.

 is _____.

23.

 is _____.

CHAPTER 3 Addition Facts to 10

Practice 1   Ways to Add

Add. Count on from the greater number.

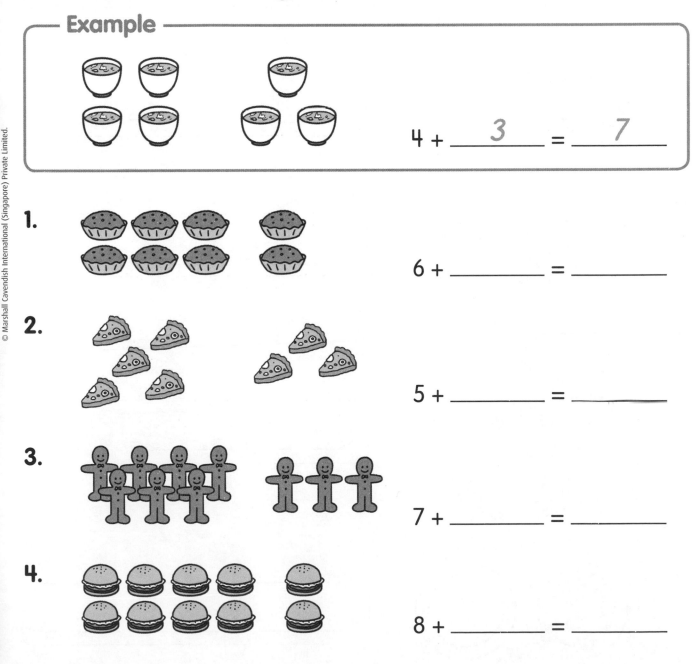

Example

$4 + \underline{\quad 3 \quad} = \underline{\quad 7 \quad}$

1.

$6 + \underline{\qquad} = \underline{\qquad}$

2.

$5 + \underline{\qquad} = \underline{\qquad}$

3.

$7 + \underline{\qquad} = \underline{\qquad}$

4.

$8 + \underline{\qquad} = \underline{\qquad}$

Look at the pictures.
Add. Count on from the greater number.

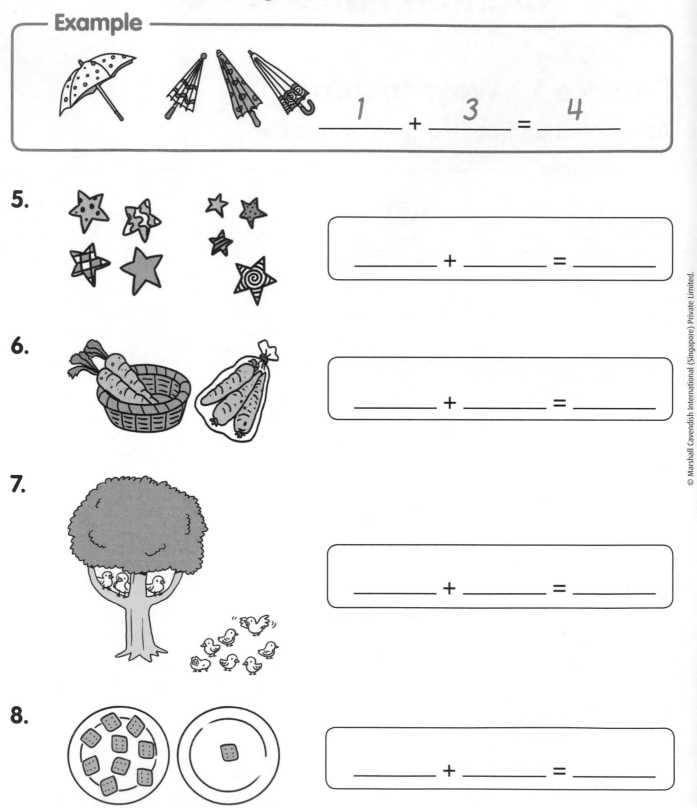

Example

_____1_____ + _____3_____ = _____4_____

5.

_____ + _____ = _____

6.

_____ + _____ = _____

7.

_____ + _____ = _____

8.

_____ + _____ = _____

Count on to add.

9.

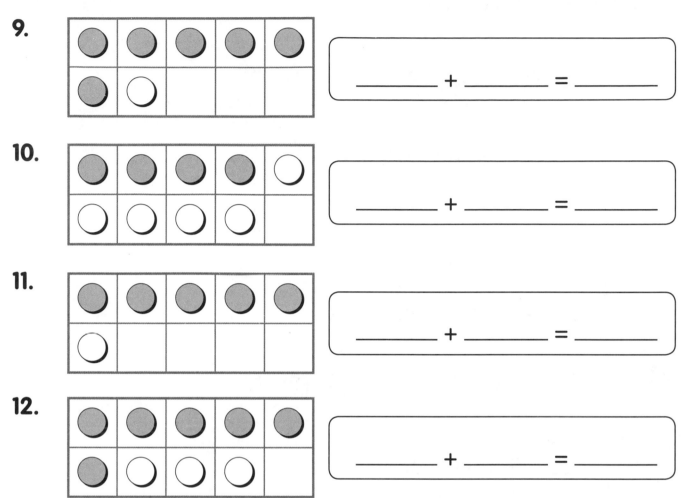

_____ + _____ = _____

10.

_____ + _____ = _____

11.

_____ + _____ = _____

12.

_____ + _____ = _____

Count on from the greater number to add.

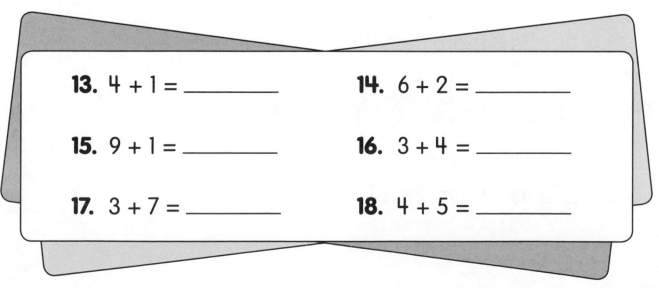

13. 4 + 1 = _____   **14.** 6 + 2 = _____

15. 9 + 1 = _____   **16.** 3 + 4 = _____

17. 3 + 7 = _____   **18.** 4 + 5 = _____

Complete.
Count on using a counting tape.

19. | 1 | 2 | 3 | 4 | 5 | 6 | 7 | 8 | 9 | 10 |

_____ is 2 more than 4.

20. | 1 | 2 | 3 | 4 | 5 | 6 | 7 | 8 | 9 | 10 |

_____ is 3 more than 5.

21. | 1 | 2 | 3 | 4 | 5 | 6 | 7 | 8 | 9 | 10 |

_____ is 4 more than 6.

22. | 1 | 2 | 3 | 4 | 5 | 6 | 7 | 8 | 9 | 10 |

_____ is 8 more than 2.

23. | 1 | 2 | 3 | 4 | 5 | 6 | 7 | 8 | 9 | 10 |

_____ is 7 more than 1.

Complete.
Write the answer in each ☐.

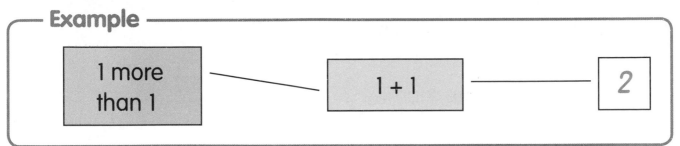

Example

| 1 more than 1 | — | 1 + 1 | — | 2 |

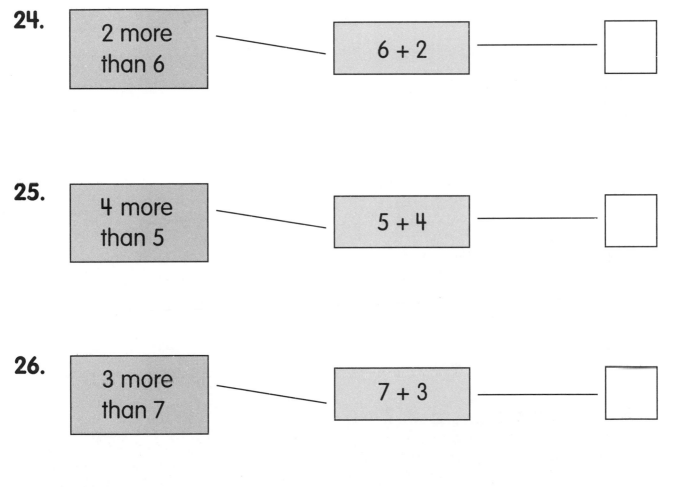

24. | 2 more than 6 | — | 6 + 2 | — | ☐ |

25. | 4 more than 5 | — | 5 + 4 | — | ☐ |

26. | 3 more than 7 | — | 7 + 3 | — | ☐ |

27. | 2 more than 8 | — | 8 + 2 | — | ☐ |

Fill in the blanks using a counting tape.

28. 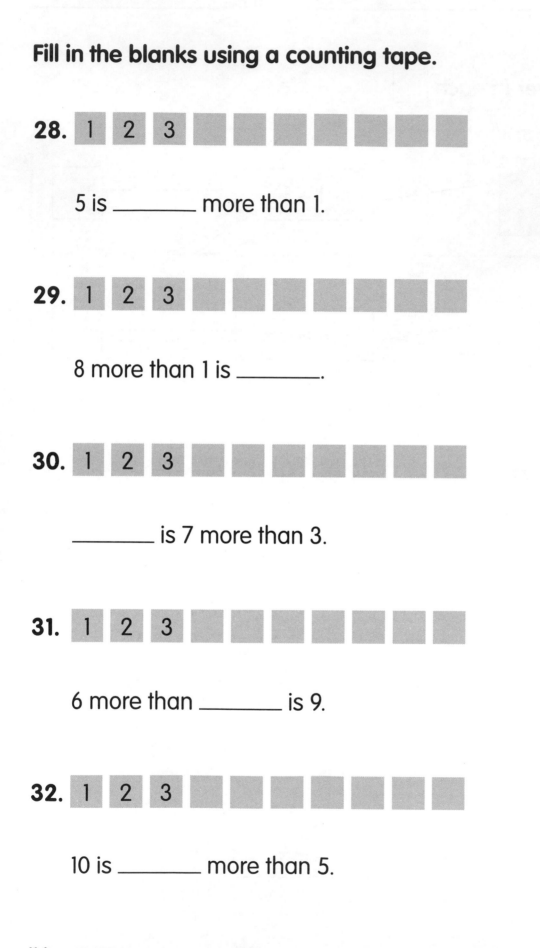 1 2 3 ▢ ▢ ▢ ▢ ▢ ▢ ▢

5 is _____ more than 1.

29. 1 2 3 ▢ ▢ ▢ ▢ ▢ ▢ ▢

8 more than 1 is _____.

30. 1 2 3 ▢ ▢ ▢ ▢ ▢ ▢ ▢

_____ is 7 more than 3.

31. 1 2 3 ▢ ▢ ▢ ▢ ▢ ▢ ▢

6 more than _____ is 9.

32. 1 2 3 ▢ ▢ ▢ ▢ ▢ ▢ ▢

10 is _____ more than 5.

Practice 2 Ways to Add

Complete the number bonds.

Then fill in the blanks.

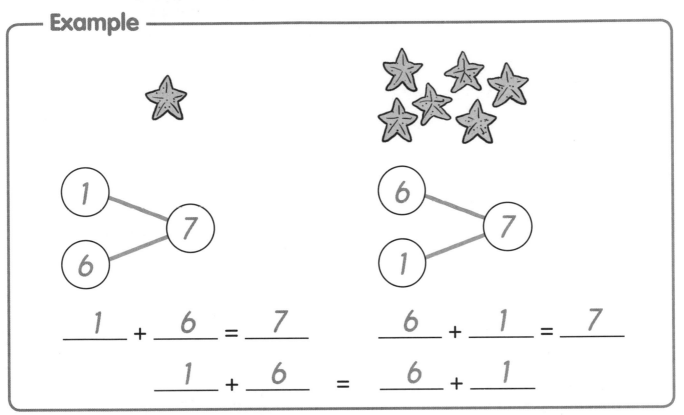

Example

_1_ + _6_ = _7_

_1_ + _6_ = _6_ + _1_

_6_ + _1_ = _7_

1.

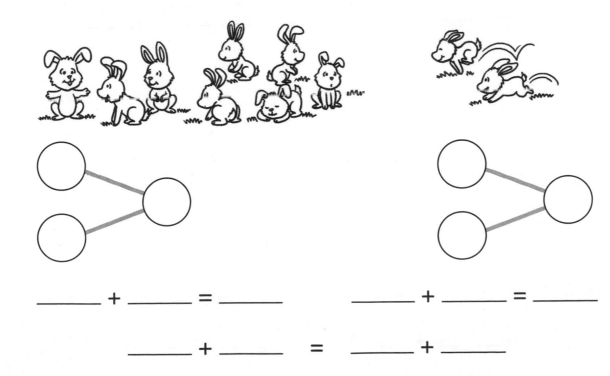

_____ + _____ = _____   _____ + _____ = _____

_____ + _____ = _____ + _____

2.

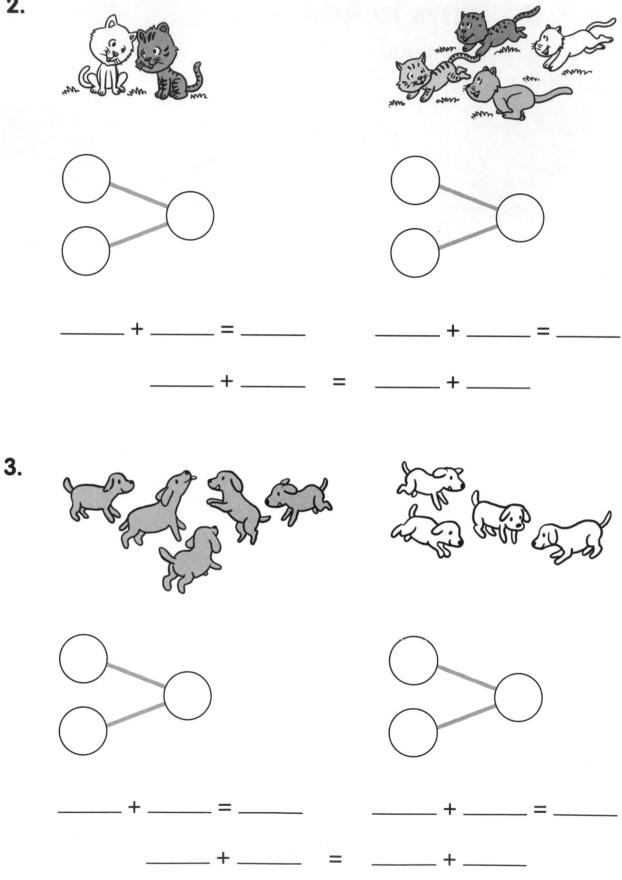

_____ + _____ = _____

_____ + _____ = _____ + _____

3.

_____ + _____ = _____

_____ + _____ = _____ + _____

Name: _____   **Date:** _____

Complete the number bonds.
Then fill in the blanks.

4. $1 + \_\_\_\_ = 5$

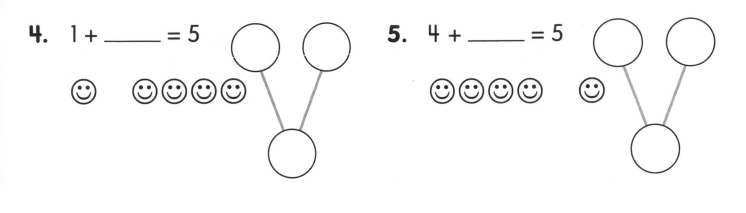

5. $4 + \_\_\_\_ = 5$

6. $\_\_\_\_ + 5 = 8$

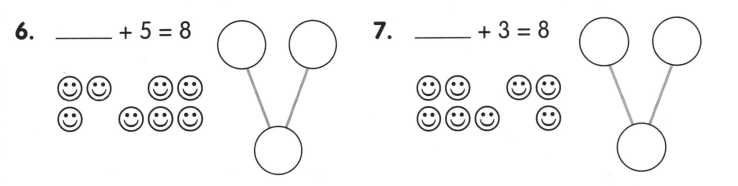

7. $\_\_\_\_ + 3 = 8$

8. $10 + \_\_\_\_ = 10$

9. $\_\_\_\_ + 10 = 10$

Help each Momma Butterfly find her babies!
Color the small butterflies that match her number.

10.

11.

12.

13.

14.

Name: _____   **Date:** _____

Add.

You can draw number bonds to help you.

15.

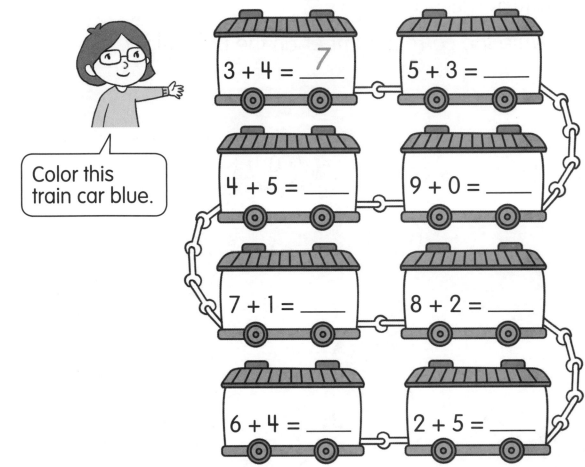

Color this train car blue.

3 + 4 = _7_   5 + 3 = _____

4 + 5 = _____   9 + 0 = _____

7 + 1 = _____   8 + 2 = _____

6 + 4 = _____   2 + 5 = _____

Now color the train cars above.

Then fill in the table with your answers.

16.

If your answer is	Color	Number of train cars
7	blue	
8	green	
9	orange	
10	red	

Solve.

17. A ball falls into the number machine.
Which ball is it?
Write the correct number on the ball below.

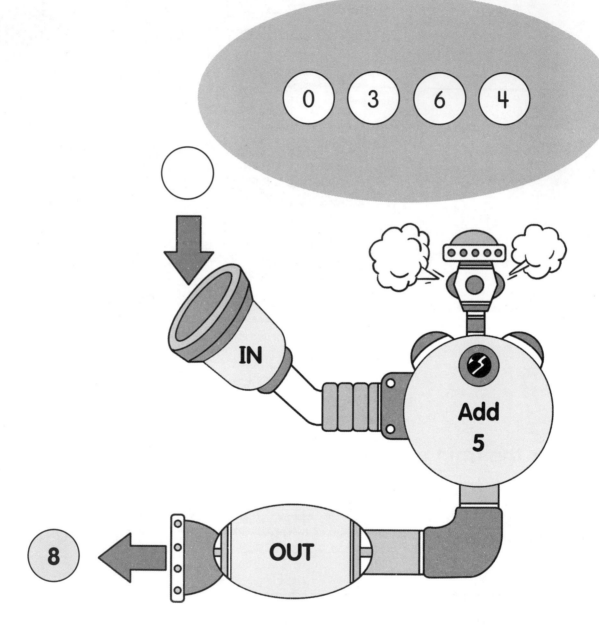

Practice 3 Making Addition Stories

Use the pictures to make addition stories.
Use number bonds to help you.

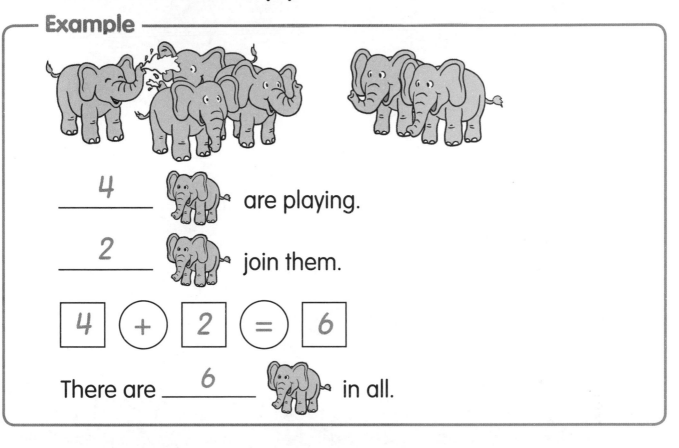

Example

_____4_____ are playing.

_____2_____ join them.

| 4 | (+) | 2 | (=) | 6 |

There are _____6_____ in all.

1.

There are _____ .

There are _____ .

☐ ○ ☐ ○ ☐

There are _____ in all.

2.

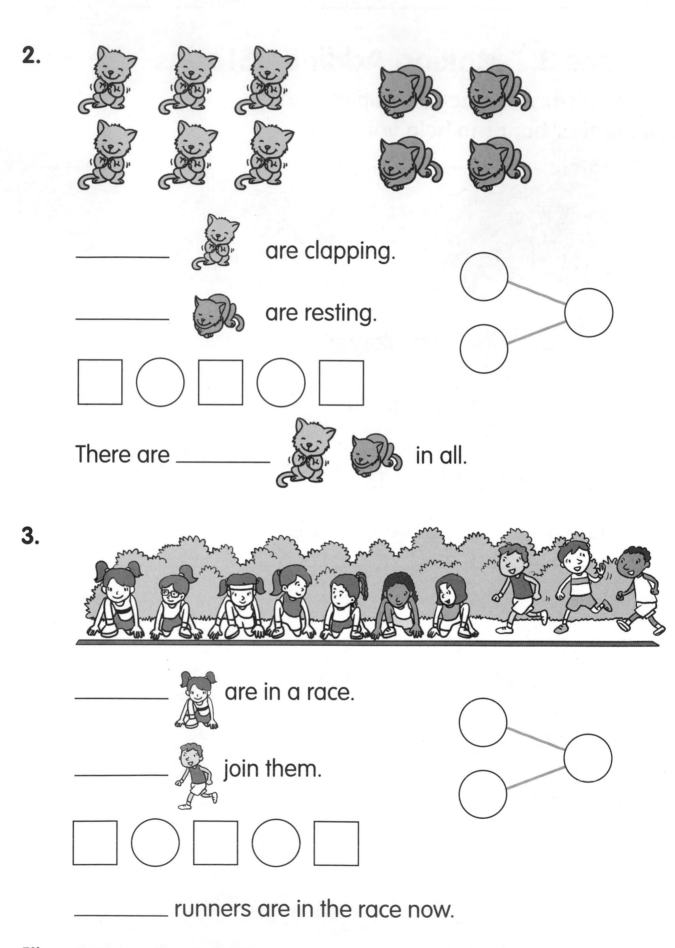

_____ are clapping.

_____ are resting.

☐ ○ ☐ ○ ☐

There are _____ in all.

3.

_____ are in a race.

_____ join them.

☐ ○ ☐ ○ ☐

_____ runners are in the race now.

4.

Sonia has _____ 🍪 .

She buys _____ ⭐ .

☐ ○ ☐ ○ ☐

Sonia has _____ ⭐🍓 in all.

5.

There are _____ 🐟 .

There are _____ 🐟 .

☐ ○ ☐ ○ ☐

There are _____ 🐟🐟 in all.

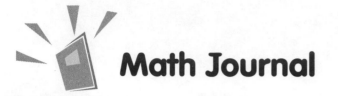

Math Journal

Write your own addition story.

Use the helping words.

Before you begin, color each group of pencils a different color.

| pencils | buys | new | pencils | in all |

_____

_____

_____

_____

☐ ◯ ☐ ◯ ☐

_____

Practice 4   Real-World Problems: Addition

Solve.
Write addition sentences to help you.

Example

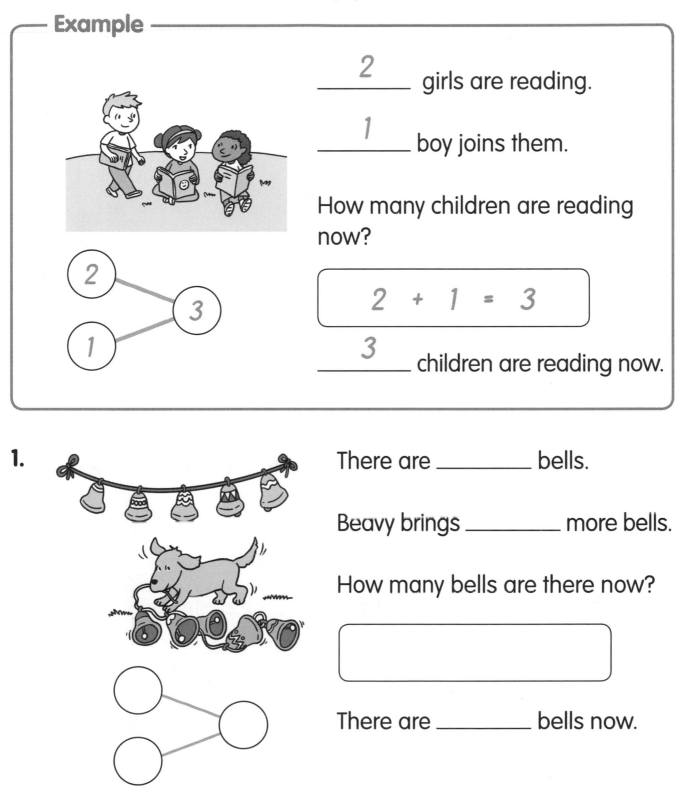

_____2_____ girls are reading.

_____1_____ boy joins them.

How many children are reading now?

| 2 | + | 1 | = | 3 |

_____3_____ children are reading now.

1.

There are _____ bells.

Beavy brings _____ more bells.

How many bells are there now?

There are _____ bells now.

2.

This toy has _____ straight legs.

It has _____ curly legs.

How many legs does the toy have in all?

○—○
○—○

The toy has _____ legs in all.

3.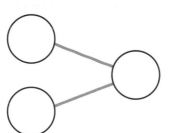

Mariah has _____ apples.

She has _____ oranges.

How many fruits does Mariah have in all?

○—○
○—○

Mariah has _____ fruits in all.

Put On Your Thinking Cap!

Challenging Practice

Solve.

Ivy and Reena have 10 prizes in all.
They do not have the same number of prizes.
How many prizes can Reena have?

There is more than one correct answer!

Reena can have _____ prizes.

© Marshall Cavendish International (Singapore) Private Limited.

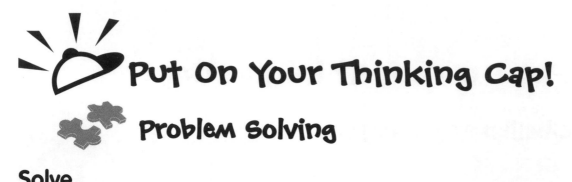

Put On Your Thinking Cap!

Problem Solving

Solve.

Lilian has these candles.
Help her choose the correct number candle for her friend's birthday.

- Cross out two numbers that add up to 5.
- Cross out two numbers that add up to 10.
- Look at the two numbers that are left.
  Cross out the number that is less.

The correct number candle is _____.

Chapter Review/Test

Vocabulary

Choose the correct word.

plus
add
equal to
more than
addition sentence

1. You can _____ by counting on from the greater number.

2. 2 + 3 = 5 is an _____.

3. 3 plus 4 is _____ 7.

4. "+" is read as _____.

5. 6 is 2 _____ 4.

Concepts and Skills

Add by counting on from the greater number.

6. 3 + 6 = _____   7. 7 + 1 = _____

8. 2 + 8 = _____   9. 1 + 9 = _____

Fill in the blanks using a counting tape.

10. _____ is 3 more than 6.

11. _____ is 2 more than 5.

12. _____ is 4 more than 4.

Look at the pictures.
Fill in the blanks.

13.

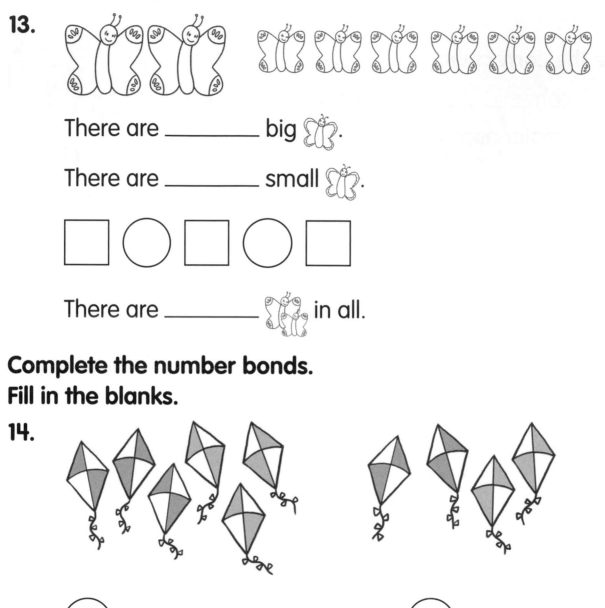

There are _____ big 🦋.

There are _____ small 🦋.

☐ ◯ ☐ ◯ ☐

There are _____ 🦋 in all.

Complete the number bonds.
Fill in the blanks.

14.

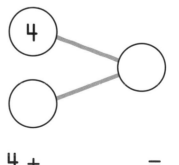

6 + _____ = _____

4 + _____ = _____

6 + 4 = 4 + _____

Problem Solving

Solve.

15. Carlos has 3 brown belts.
He has 2 black belts.
How many belts does he have in all?

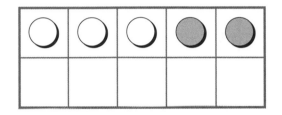

$3 + 2 =$ _____

Carlos has _____ belts in all.

16. Jane has 4 bows.
She gets 3 more bows.
How many bows does she have now?

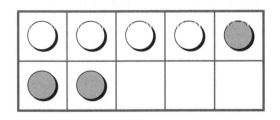

$4 + 3 =$ _____

Jane has _____ bows now.

Draw .
Then solve.

17. How many toys are there in all?

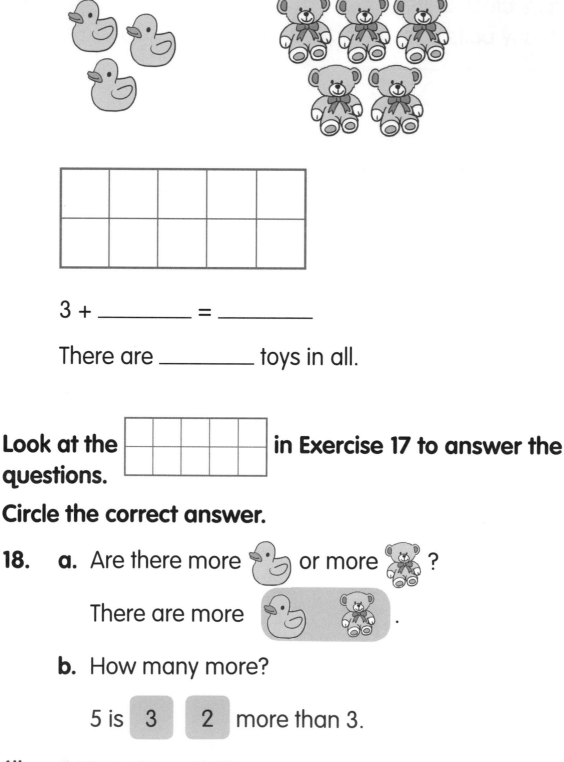

3 + _____ = _____

There are _____ toys in all.

Look at the ▭▭▭▭▭ **in Exercise 17 to answer the**
questions.

Circle the correct answer.

18. **a.** Are there more 🦆 or more 🧸 ?

There are more (🦆 🧸) .

b. How many more?

5 is [3] [2] more than 3.

CHAPTER 4 Subtraction Facts to 10

Practice 1 Ways To Subtract

Cross out to subtract.
Then circle the answer.

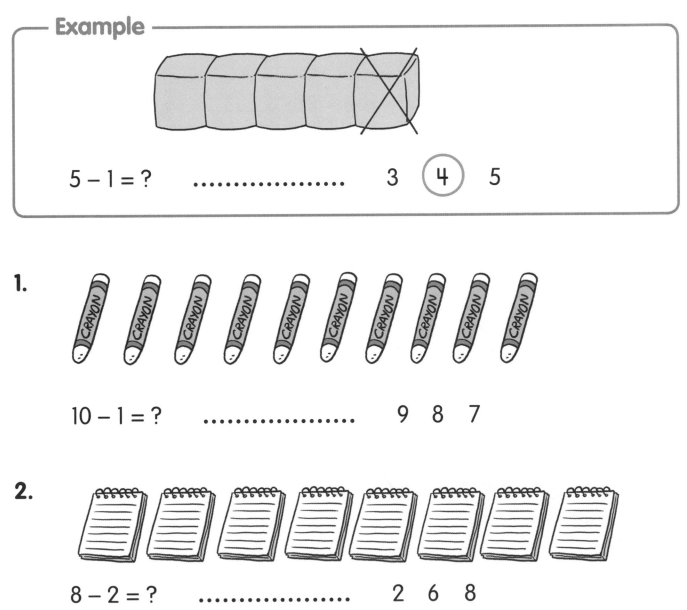

┌─ **Example** ──────────────────────────────────┐

$5 - 1 = ?$ 3 (**4**) 5

└──┘

1.

$10 - 1 = ?$ 9 8 7

2.

$8 - 2 = ?$ 2 6 8

Write a subtraction sentence for each picture.

Example

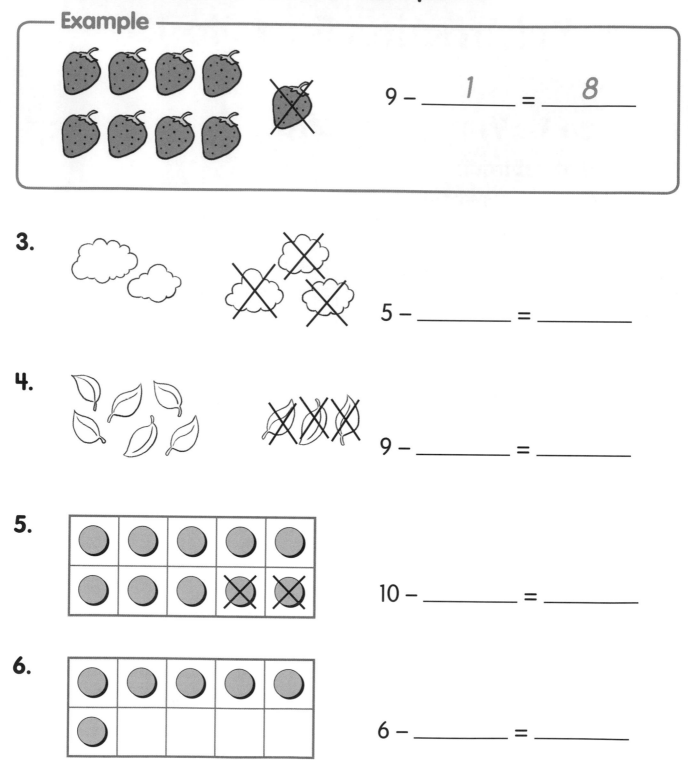

$9 - \underline{\quad 1 \quad} = \underline{\quad 8 \quad}$

3.

$5 - \underline{\qquad} = \underline{\qquad}$

4.

$9 - \underline{\qquad} = \underline{\qquad}$

5.

$10 - \underline{\qquad} = \underline{\qquad}$

6.

$6 - \underline{\qquad} = \underline{\qquad}$

Name: _____ **Date:** _____

Complete.

┌─ Example ─────────────────────────────────────

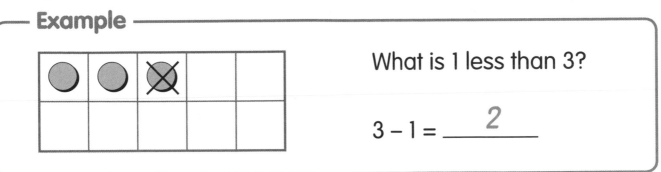

What is 1 less than 3?

$3 - 1 =$ _____ 2

7.

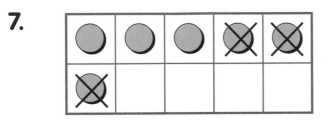

What is 3 less than 6?

$6 - 3 =$ _____

Cross out to subtract.
Then write the subtraction sentence.

┌─ Example ─────────────────────────────────────

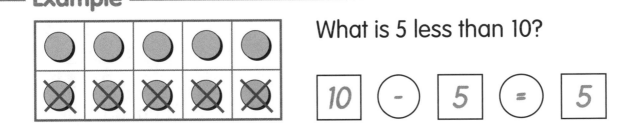

What is 5 less than 10?

10 (–) 5 (=) 5

8.   What is 4 less than 7?

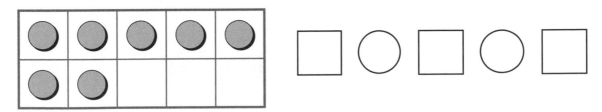

Cross out to subtract.
Then write the subtraction sentence.

9. What is 2 less than 9?

   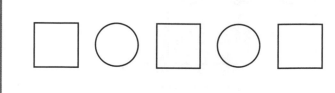

Subtract.
Count on from the number that is less.
Fill in the blanks.

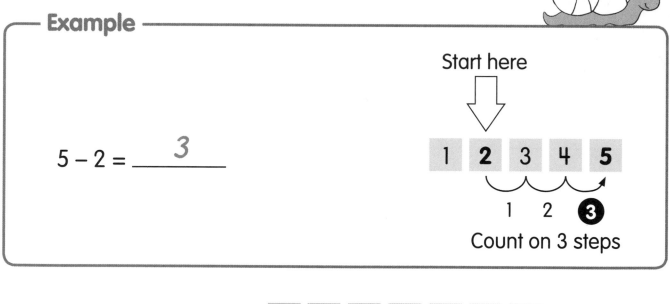

── Example ──

$5 - 2 =$ _____ *3*

Start here

Count on 3 steps

1 **2** 3 4 **5**

1 2 **3**

10. $7 - 4 =$ _____   1 2 3 4 5 6 7

11. $5 - 3 =$ _____   1 2 3 4 5

12. $8 - 4 =$ _____   1 2 3 4 5 6 7 8

Count back from the greater number to subtract. Fill in the blanks.

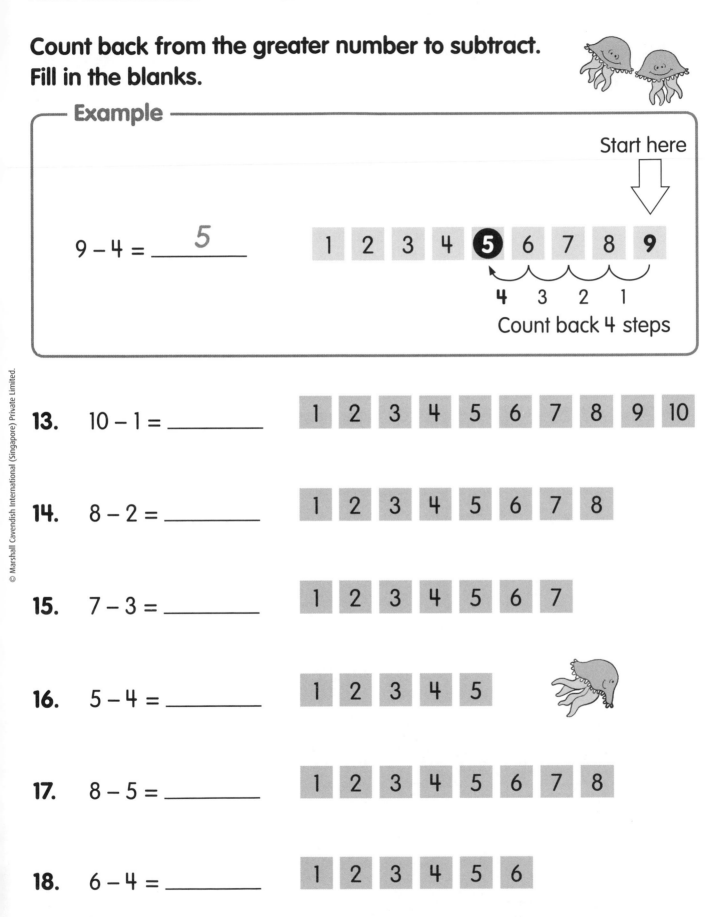

Example

Start here

$9 - 4 =$ ___5___

| 1 | 2 | 3 | 4 | **5** | 6 | 7 | 8 | **9** |

4 3 2 1

Count back 4 steps

13. $10 - 1 =$ _____

| 1 | 2 | 3 | 4 | 5 | 6 | 7 | 8 | 9 | 10 |

14. $8 - 2 =$ _____

| 1 | 2 | 3 | 4 | 5 | 6 | 7 | 8 |

15. $7 - 3 =$ _____

| 1 | 2 | 3 | 4 | 5 | 6 | 7 |

16. $5 - 4 =$ _____

| 1 | 2 | 3 | 4 | 5 |

17. $8 - 5 =$ _____

| 1 | 2 | 3 | 4 | 5 | 6 | 7 | 8 |

18. $6 - 4 =$ _____

| 1 | 2 | 3 | 4 | 5 | 6 |

Color the correct shape.

Example

19.

20.

21.

22.

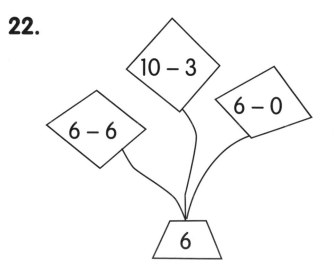

Practice 2   Ways To Subtract

Fill in each number bond.
Then complete the subtraction sentence.

Example

5 – 1 = ___4___

1.

6 – 3 = _____

2.

7 – 4 = _____

3.

$8 - 3 =$ _____

4.

$9 - 3 =$ _____

5.

$10 - 8 =$ _____

Fill in the number bonds.
Then write the missing numbers in the subtraction sentences.

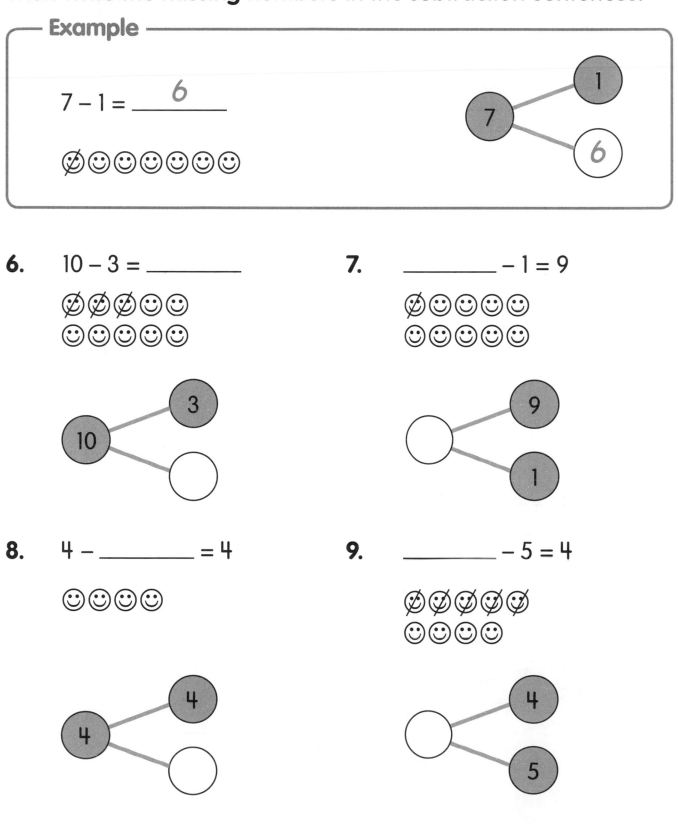

Example

$7 - 1 =$ _____ *6*

6. $10 - 3 =$ _____

7. _____ $- 1 = 9$

8. $4 -$ _____ $= 4$

9. _____ $- 5 = 4$

Some stickers are torn off.
Write a subtraction sentence to find how many are left.

Example

10 _____ – _____ 4 = _____ 6

10.

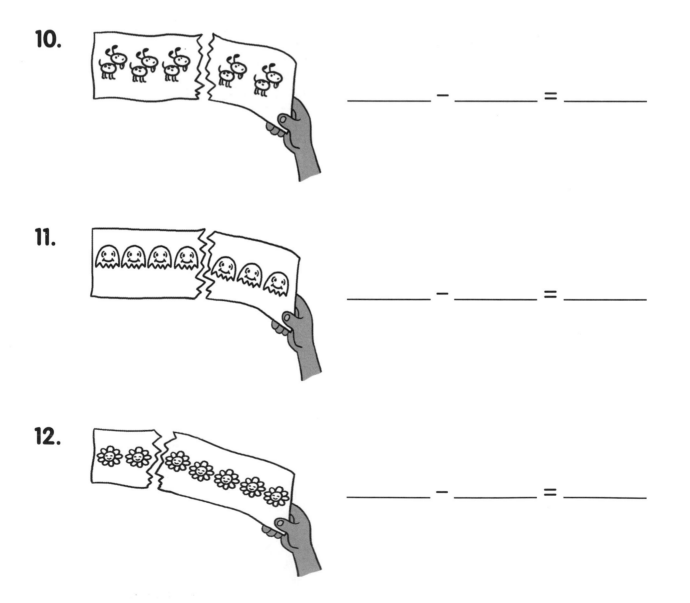

_____ – _____ = _____

11.

_____ – _____ = _____

12.

_____ – _____ = _____

Subtract.
Then match the answers to show where each animal lives.

13.

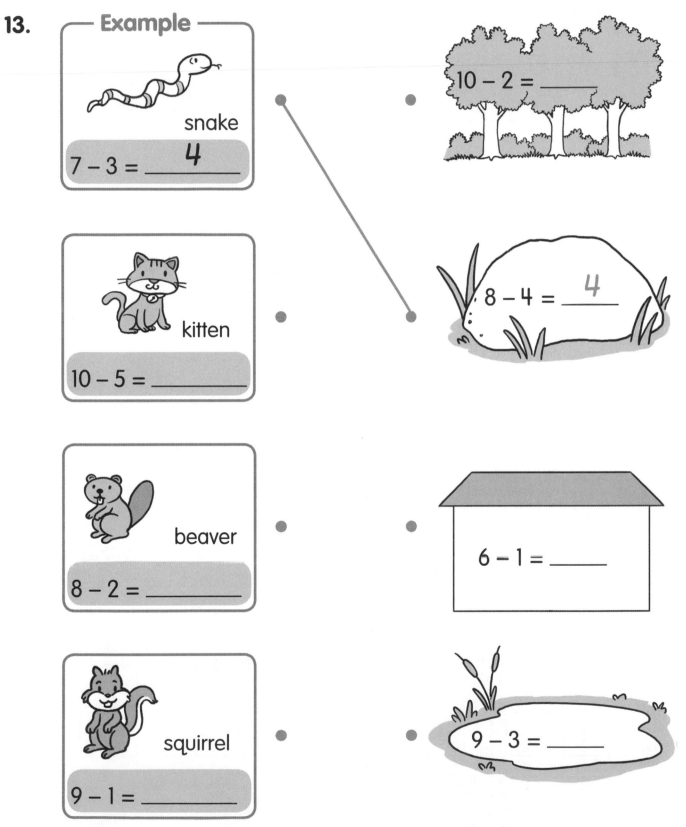

Example

snake

$7 - 3 =$ ___4___

kitten

$10 - 5 =$ _____

beaver

$8 - 2 =$ _____

squirrel

$9 - 1 =$ _____

$10 - 2 =$ _____

$8 - 4 =$ ___4___

$6 - 1 =$ _____

$9 - 3 =$ _____

Complete.

Then write the letters in the correct ☐ **to solve the riddle.**

14. $10 - 5 =$ _____ 5 **R**

15. $9 - 8 =$ _____ **I**

16. $6 - 3 =$ _____ **B**

17. $7 - 5 =$ _____ **S**

18. $9 - 4 =$ _____ **R**

19. $10 - 0 =$ _____ **A**

20. $9 - 1 =$ _____ **E**

21. $6 - 2 =$ _____ **V**

22. $10 - 3 =$ _____ **K**

23. $9 - 0 =$ _____ **N**

Where do fish keep their money?

In	R	☐	☐	☐	☐		☐	☐	☐	☐	☐
5	1	4	8	5		3	10	9	7	2

Name: _____ Date: _____

Practice 3   Making Subtraction Stories

Look at the pictures.
Make subtraction stories.
Write subtraction sentences for each story.

Example

There are ___8___ pumpkins.

Jesse takes ___2___ pumpkins away.

[8] (-) [2] (=) [6]

___6___ pumpkins are left.

8 — 2, 6

1.

There are _____ children.

_____ children wear glasses.

☐ ◯ ☐ ◯ ☐

_____ children do not wear glasses.

2.

There are _____ mice.

All the mice run away.

□ ○ □ ○ □

_____ mice are left.

3.

There are _____ flowers.

_____ flowers are tulips.

□ ○ □ ○ □

_____ flowers are roses.

4.

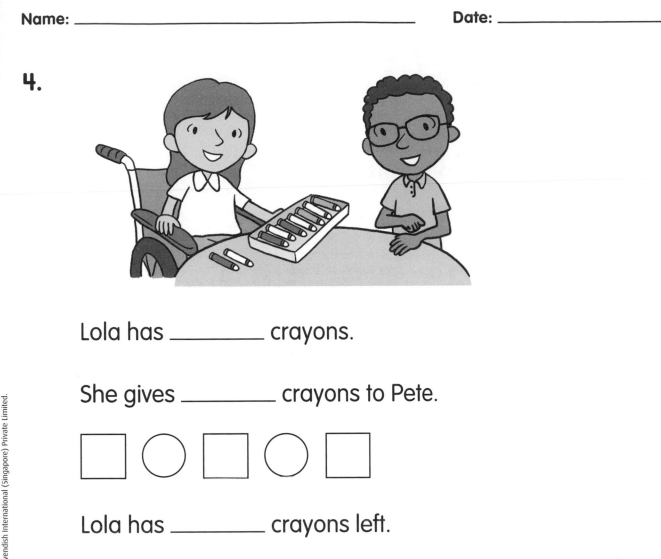

Lola has _____ crayons.

She gives _____ crayons to Pete.

☐ ○ ☐ ○ ☐

Lola has _____ crayons left.

Math Journal

Color some bunnies brown.
Then make a subtraction sentence.

1.   Sally has 9 bunnies.

_____ bunnies are brown.
How many bunnies are white?

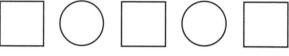

_____ bunnies are white.

Draw some balls in the drawer.
Cross some out.
Then make a subtraction sentence.

2.   Jane has _____ balls.

Her dog chews _____ of the balls.

How many balls does she have left?

Jane has _____ balls left.

Practice 4   Real-World Problems: Subtraction

Solve.

Example

There are 5 people.
1 person walks away.
How many people are left?

$$5 - 1 = 4$$

There are _____4_____ people left.

1.

Kate has 7 buttons.
None of them are white.
How many black buttons are there?

There are _____ black buttons.

2.

8 crabs are on the beach.
2 crabs crawl away.
How many crabs are left?

_____ crabs are left.

Solve.

3.

Brian has 9 toys.
6 of them are cars and the rest are bears.
How many bears does Brian have?

Brian has _____ bears.

4.

There are 10 eggs in a basket.
3 eggs roll out.
How many eggs are left?

_____ eggs are left.

5.

Abby blows 4 soap bubbles.
She pops all of them.
How many bubbles are left?

_____ bubbles are left.

Practice 5   Making Fact Families

Write a fact family for each picture.

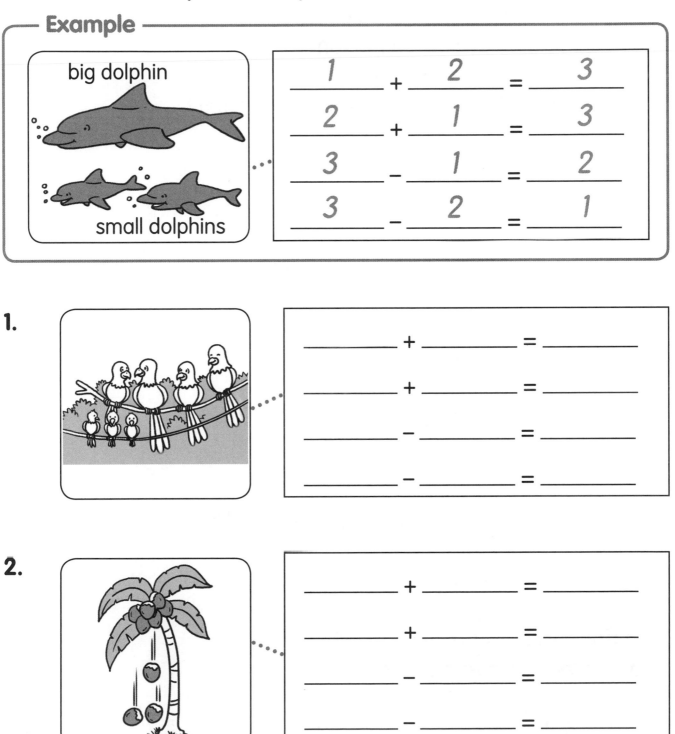

Example

big dolphin

small dolphins

1	+	2	=	3
2	+	1	=	3
3	−	1	=	2
3	−	2	=	1

1.

_____ + _____ = _____

_____ + _____ = _____

_____ − _____ = _____

_____ − _____ = _____

2.

_____ + _____ = _____

_____ + _____ = _____

_____ − _____ = _____

_____ − _____ = _____

Solve.
Use related facts to help you.

3. Simone has some tomatoes.
    She throws away 5 rotten tomatoes.
    She has 4 tomatoes left.
    How many tomatoes did she have at first?

    $\boxed{} - 5 = 4$

    $5 + 4 = \boxed{}$ is the related addition fact.

    She had _____ tomatoes at first.

4. Marcus has 6 magnets.
    Susan gives him some magnets.
    Marcus now has 9 magnets.
    How many magnets did Susan give Marcus?

    $6 + \boxed{} = 9$

    $9 - 6 = \boxed{}$ is the related subtraction fact.

    Susan gave Marcus _____ magnets.

Find the missing number.
Use related facts to help you.

5. $\boxed{} + 5 = 10$ 6. $2 + \boxed{} = 7$

7. $\boxed{} - 8 = 2$ 8. $9 - \boxed{} = 3$

Is the number sentence true or false?
Circle the correct answer.

9. $5 + 4 = 9$ true   false

10. $2 + 8 = 10$ true   false

11. $7 - 2 = 4$ true   false

12. $6 - 3 = 3$ true   false

13. $3 + 6 = 8$ true   false

14     $9 - 3 = 5$ true   false

15. $7 - 5 = 2$ true   false

16. $4 + 6 = 10$ true   false

17. $10 - 5 = 6$ true   false

18. $8 + 0 = 8$ true   false

Name: _____   **Date:** _____

Put On Your Thinking Cap!

Challenging Practice

Pick three numbers to make a fact family.
Then write each fact family.

1.

2.

Put On Your Thinking Cap!

Read this riddle.

Example

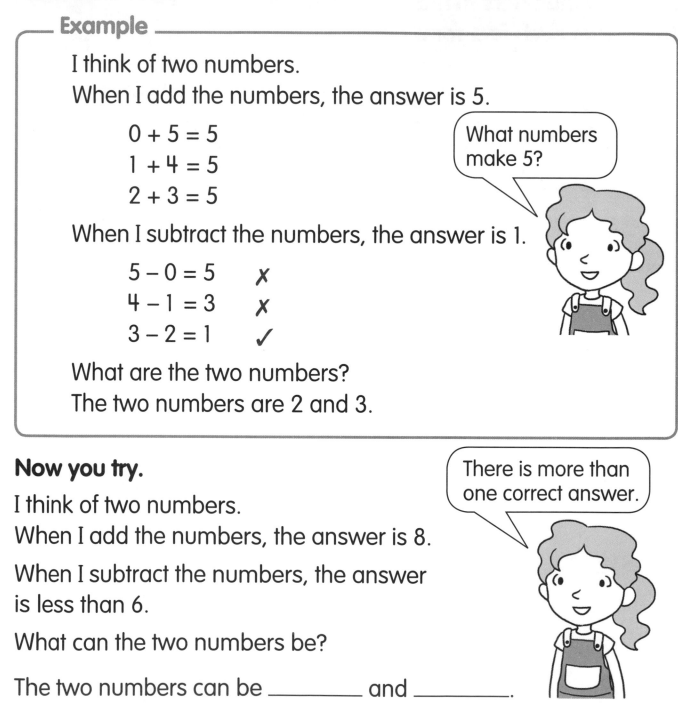

I think of two numbers.
When I add the numbers, the answer is 5.

$$0 + 5 = 5$$
$$1 + 4 = 5$$
$$2 + 3 = 5$$

What numbers make 5?

When I subtract the numbers, the answer is 1.

$5 - 0 = 5$ ✗
$4 - 1 = 3$ ✗
$3 - 2 = 1$ ✓

What are the two numbers?
The two numbers are 2 and 3.

Now you try.

There is more than one correct answer.

I think of two numbers.

When I add the numbers, the answer is 8.

When I subtract the numbers, the answer is less than 6.

What can the two numbers be?

The two numbers can be _____ and _____.

Chapter Review/Test

Vocabulary

Choose the correct word.

1. + is plus, − is _____.

2. 3 is _____ 7.

3. 7 + 2 = 9 is a _____ number sentence.

4. 4 − 3 = 1 is a _____.

> subtraction
> sentence
> _____
> true
> _____
> minus
> _____
> less than

Concepts and Skills

Complete each subtraction sentence.

5.

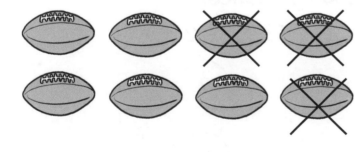

8 − _____ = _____

6. What is 4 less than 6?

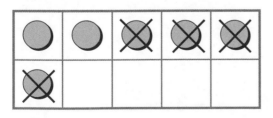

6 − _____ = _____

7. What is 3 less than 9?

9 – _____ = _____

Count on from the number which is less.

8. 6 – 3 = _____

9. 9 – 7 = _____

Count back from the greater number.

10. 10 – 5 = _____

11. 7 – 6 = _____

Complete the number bond.
Then complete the subtraction sentence.

12. 7 – 2 = ?

7 – 2 = _____

13. ? – 2 = 8

_____ – 2 = 8

Subtract.
Use related facts.

14. 8 – 4 = _____

15. 7 – 3 = _____

16. 10 – _____ = 7

17. 5 – _____ = 5

Is the number sentence true or false?
Circle the correct answer.

18. $10 - 3 = 7$ true   false

19. $5 + 3 = 9$ true   false

Write a subtraction story.

20.

_____

_____

_____

_____ − _____ = _____

_____

Write a fact family.

21 .

_____ + _____ = _____

_____ + _____ = _____

_____ − _____ = _____

_____ − _____ = _____

Problem Solving

Draw ●.

Cross them out to solve.

Then write a number sentence.

22. James has 9 fish in his fish tank.
He gives his friend 4 fish.
How many fish does he have left?

_____ − _____ = _____

James has _____ fish left.

Solve.

Use related facts to help you.

23 . Mr. Peterson bakes 10 pies.
He eats some of them.
He now has 8 pies.
How many pies did he eat?

10 − _____ = 8

Mr. Peterson ate _____ pies.

Name: _____   Date: _____

Cumulative Review

for Chapters 3 and 4

Concepts and Skills

Look at the pictures.
Complete the number sentences.

1.

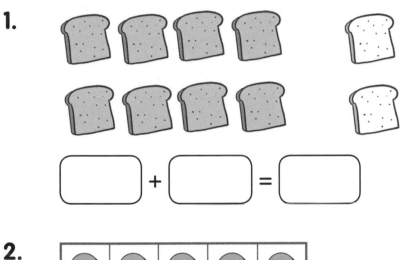

$$\boxed{} + \boxed{} = \boxed{}$$

2.

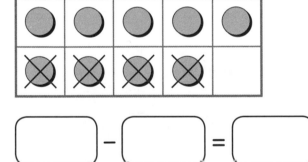

$$\boxed{} - \boxed{} = \boxed{}$$

Complete the number bonds.
Fill in the blanks.

3.   _____ + 5 = 10   4.   8 – 3 = _____

        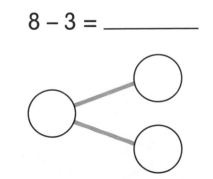

Fill in the blanks.

5. 2 more than 8 is _____.

6. 3 less than 7 is _____.

7. _____ is 2 more than 5.

8. _____ is 5 less than 10.

Find the missing number.
Use related facts to help you.

9. 2 + _____ = 8

10. _____ − 6 = 0

Pick three numbers and make a fact family.

11.

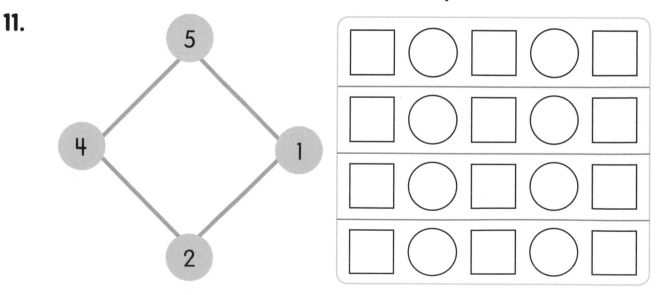

Problem Solving
Look at the pictures.
Write an addition or subtraction story.

12.

There are _____ .

There are _____ .

	◯		◯	

There are _____ in all.

13.

There are _____ .

Jamal lets go of _____ .

	◯		◯	

_____ are left.

Solve.

Write addition or subtraction sentences.

14. Ellen has 3 spoons.
Her sister gives her 5 spoons.
How many spoons does Ellen have now?

Ellen has _____ spoons now.

15. There are 8 fish in a fish tank.
6 are angelfish and the rest are goldfish.
How many goldfish are there?

There are _____ goldfish.

CHAPTER 5 Shapes and Patterns

Practice 1   Exploring Plane Shapes

Trace the dots.
Then match each shape to its name.

1.

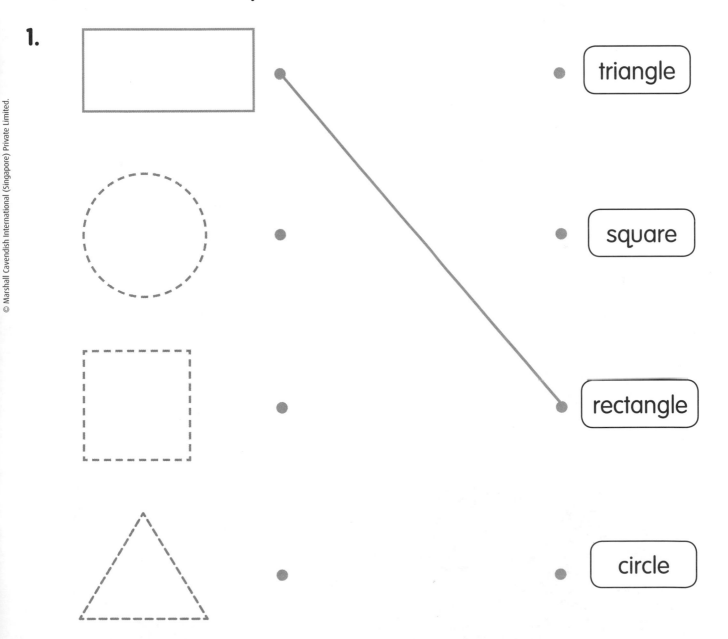

A part of each shape is missing.
Think about what shape it was.
Then match the shape to its name.

2.

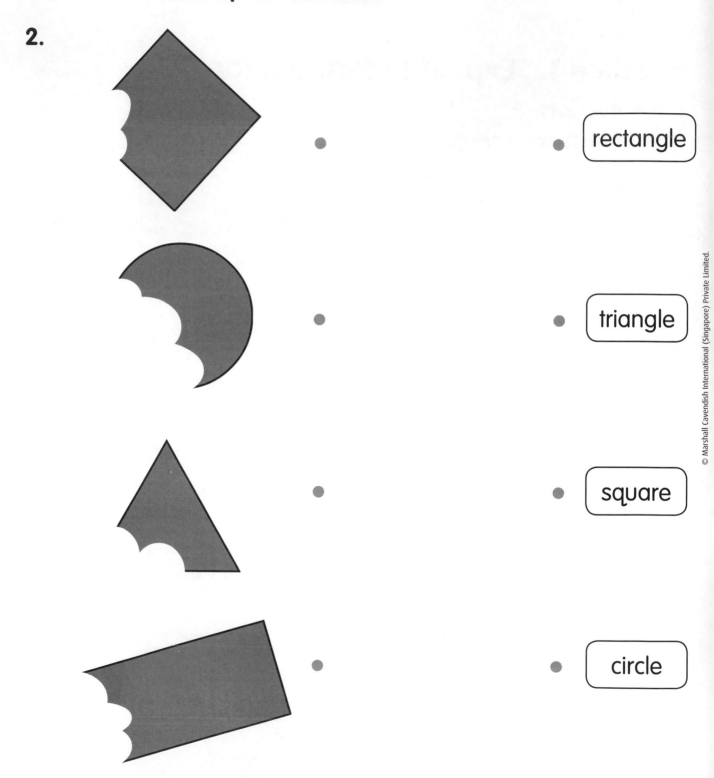

rectangle

triangle

square

circle

Circle the shapes that are the same shape as the shaded shape.

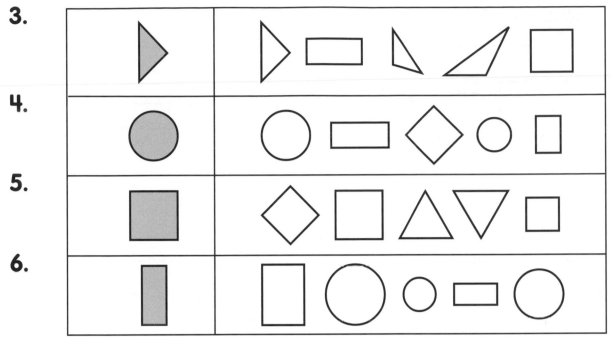

3.

4.

5.

6.

Color the shapes.

7. squares

8. triangles

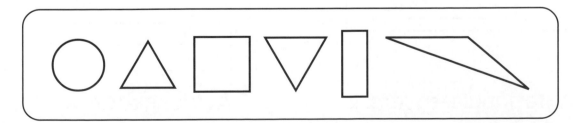

Color the shapes.

9. rectangles

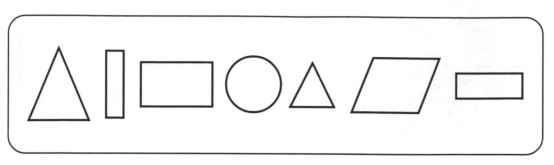

10. The shapes that are <u>not</u> circles.

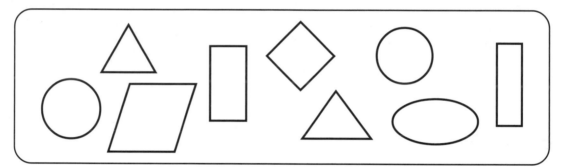

Which shape is <u>not</u> in each set?
Circle the correct answer.

11.

Set A

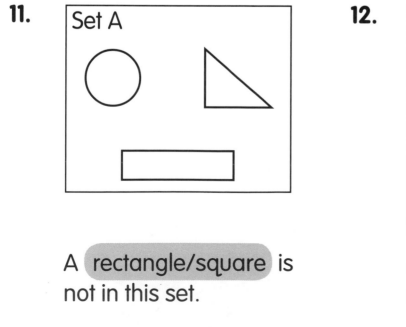

A rectangle/square is
not in this set.

12.

Set B

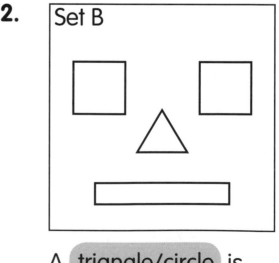

A triangle/circle is
not in this set.

Name: _____ **Date:** _____

How many sides and corners are there?
Count.

13.

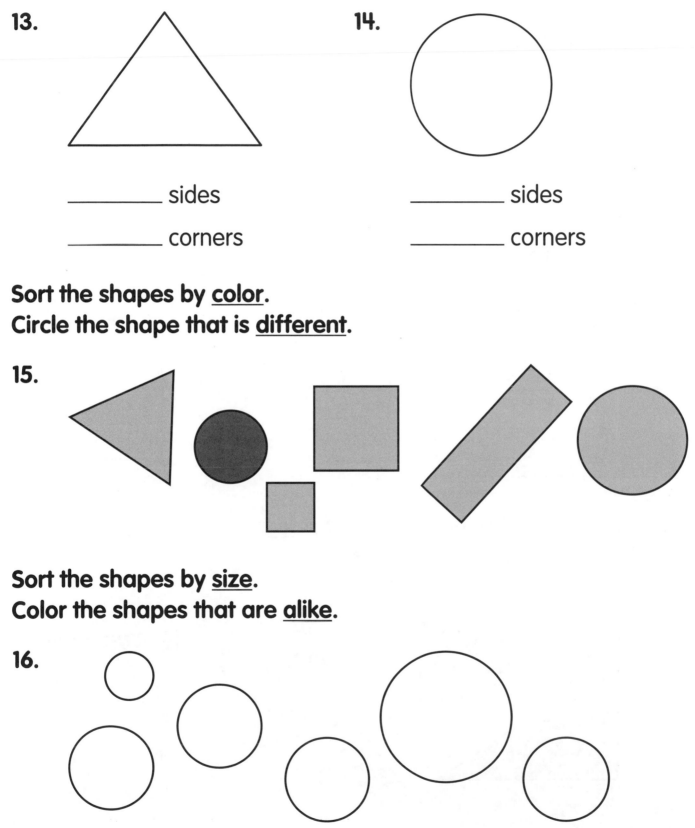

_____ sides

_____ corners

14.

_____ sides

_____ corners

Sort the shapes by <u>color</u>.
Circle the shape that is <u>different</u>.

15.

Sort the shapes by <u>size</u>.
Color the shapes that are <u>alike</u>.

16.

Sort the shapes by <u>shape</u>.
Color the shapes that are <u>alike</u>.

17.

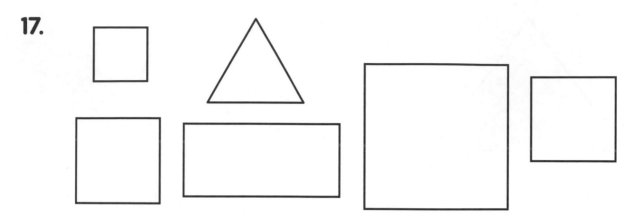

Sort the shapes by <u>corners</u>.
Circle the shape that is <u>different</u>.

18.

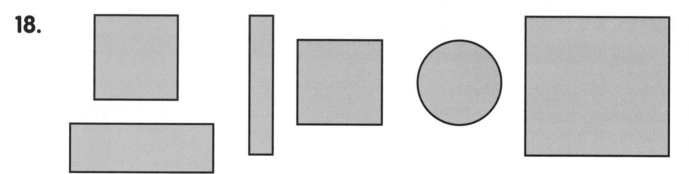

Sort the shapes by the <u>number of sides</u>.
Circle the shape that is <u>different</u>.

19.

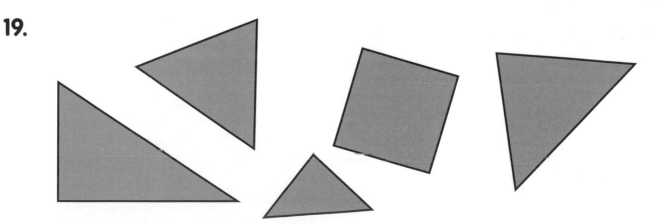

Practice 2   Exploring Plane Shapes

Read.
Then answer the questions.

1.   Josh has a square piece of paper.
He folds it and unfolds it.
Then he draws a line along the fold.
Now he has two new shapes, A and B.

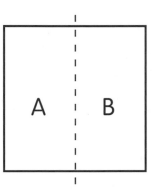

Write *yes* or *no*.

a.   Are Shape A and Shape B the same shape? _____

b.   Are Shape A and Shape B the same size? _____

Count.

c.   How many sides are there?

Shape A _____   Shape B _____

d.   How many corners are there?

Shape A _____   Shape B _____

Write *yes* or *no*.

    e.   Are Shape A and Shape B <u>different</u>? _____

Josh then cuts out Shape A and Shape B.

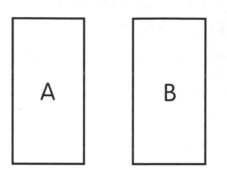

    f.   Can Shape A fit exactly over Shape B? _____

Are the shapes the <u>same</u> shape and size?
Write *yes* or *no*.

2.

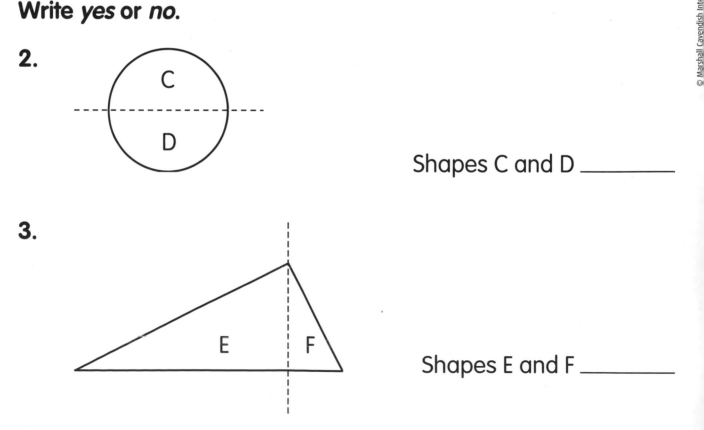

Shapes C and D _____

3.

Shapes E and F _____

Circle the correct answer.

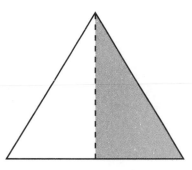

4.   The triangle is made up of two / three equal parts.

5.   One half of / fourth of the triangle is shaded.

Circle the correct answer.

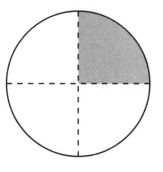

6.   The circle is made up of three / four equal parts.

7.   One half of / fourth of the circle is shaded.

Which rectangle is cut into halves?
Check your answer.

8.

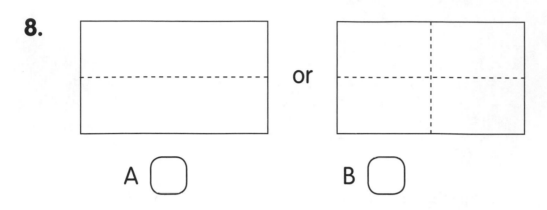

A ◯   B ◯

Fill in the blank.

9.   Which rectangle in Exercise 8 has bigger parts, A or B?

Rectangle _____ has bigger parts.

Color 1 quarter of the circle blue.

10 .

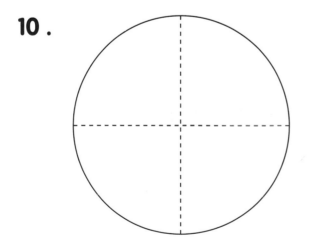

Practice 3   Exploring Solid Shapes

Match each shape to its name.

1.

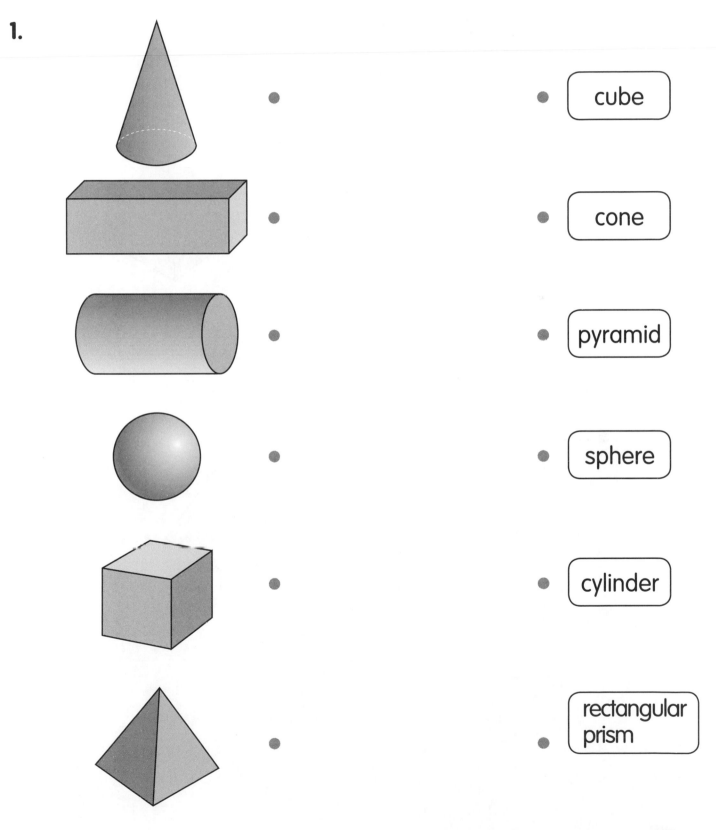

- cube
- cone
- pyramid
- sphere
- cylinder
- rectangular prism

Answer the questions.
Circle the shapes.

2.   Which shapes are <u>not</u> cylinders?

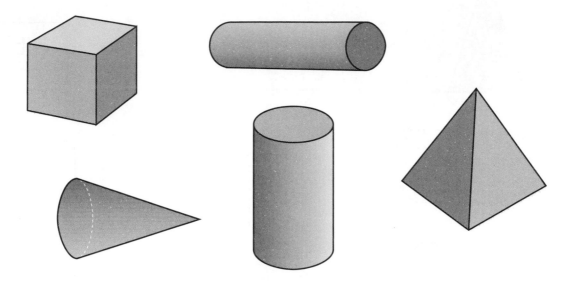

3.   Which shapes are <u>not</u> pyramids?

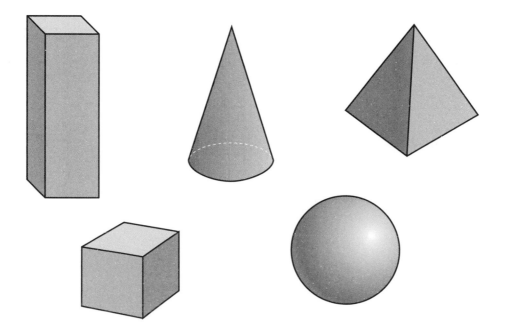

Answer the questions.
Circle the shapes.

4.   Which shapes can you stack?

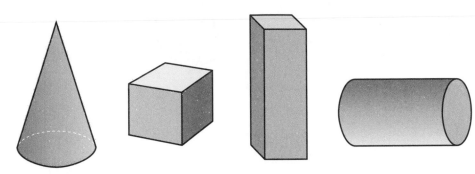

5.   Which shapes can you slide?

6.   Which shapes can you roll?

7. Which shape can you <u>only</u> slide?

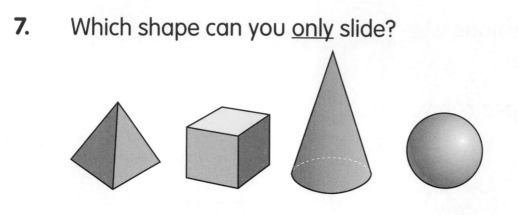

8. Which shape can you <u>only</u> roll?

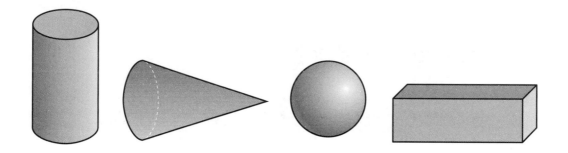

Practice 4   Making Pictures and Models with Shapes

Find the shapes in the pictures.
Count how many of each shape there are.
Write the number.

1.

Shape		Number
△	triangle	3
○	circle	
▭	rectangle	
□	square	

2.

Shape		Number
△	triangle	
○	circle	
▭	rectangle	
□	square	

Match the pieces to make a shape.
Name the shapes.
Use the words in the box.

circle
square
triangle
rectangle

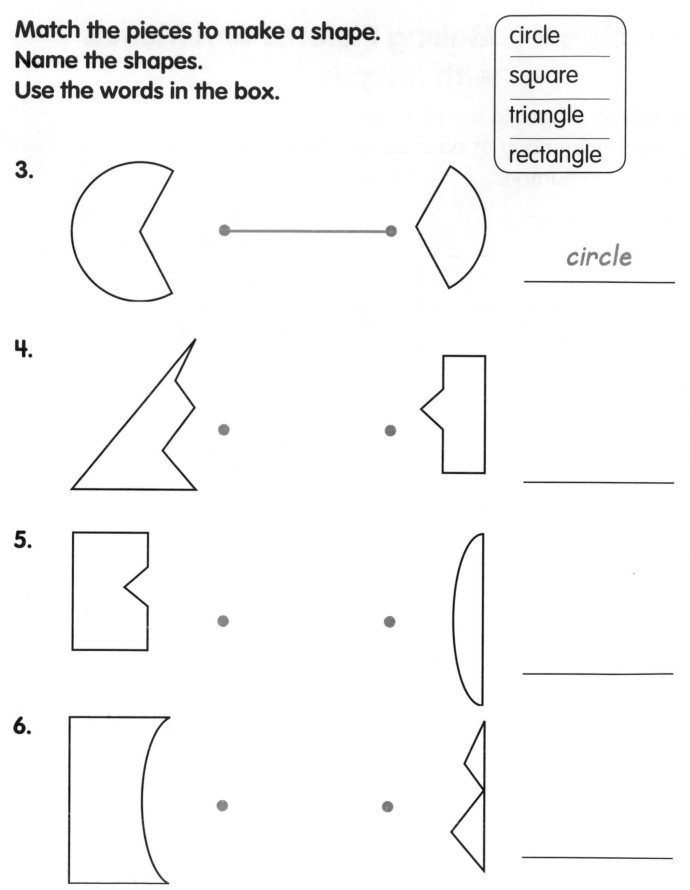

3. _circle_

4. _____

5. _____

6. _____

Name: _____ **Date:** _____

Cut out the shapes below and make a picture. Paste the picture here or use your own paper. You do not need to use all the shapes.

7.

Name: _____   **Date:** _____

Look at the pictures.
Then fill in the blanks.

8.   How many triangles can you see?

I can see _____ triangles.

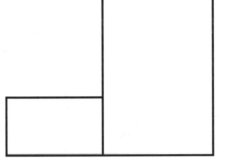

9.   A star can be made of triangles.

This star is made of _____ triangles.

Draw triangles another way to make up this star.

This star is made of _____ triangles.

10. Draw a picture with shapes.
Count how many of each shape there are.
Write the number.

Shape		Number
△	triangle	
○	circle	
▭	rectangle	
☐	square	

Practice 5 Making Pictures and Models with Shapes

Look at the pictures.
Count how many of each solid shape there are.
Write the number.

1.

Shape		Number
●	sphere	
▮	cylinder	
▭	rectangular prism	
▲	cone	
◻	cube	
◢	pyramid	

2.

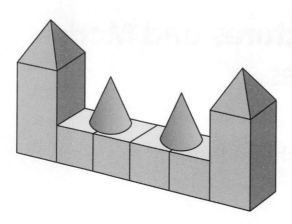

Shape		Number
⬤	sphere	
▯	cylinder	
▱	rectangular prism	
△	cone	
◰	cube	
◮	pyramid	

3.

Shape		Number
⬤	sphere	
▯	cylinder	
▱	rectangular prism	
△	cone	
◰	cube	
◮	pyramid	

Practice 6 Seeing Shapes Around Us

Trace the shape of each thing.
Then color.

1.

| ● Circles - red | ■ Squares - yellow |
| ▲ Triangles - blue | ▬ Rectangles - green |

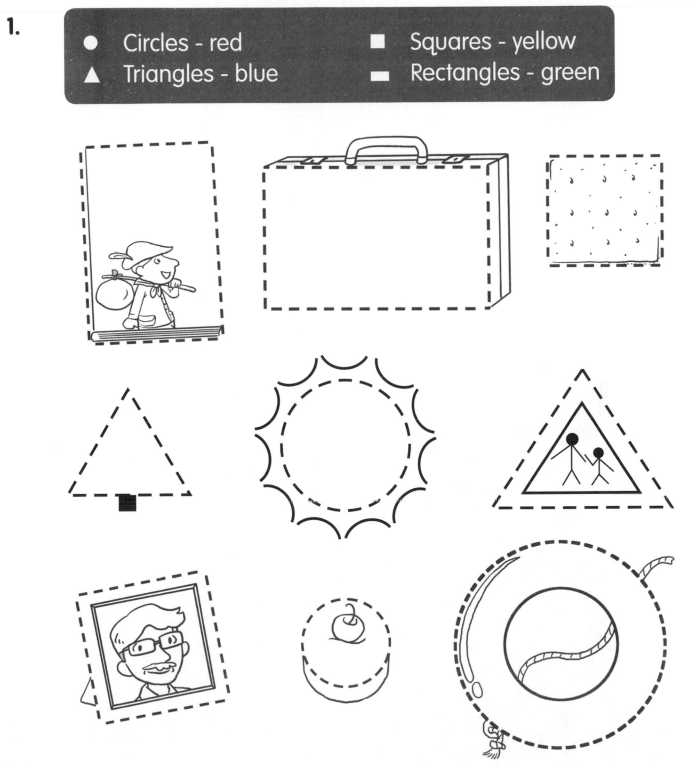

Look at the pictures.
Circle the correct things.

2. the thing that has the shape of a square

3. the thing that does <u>not</u> have the shape of a circle

Keep
Your
School
Clean

Match.

4.

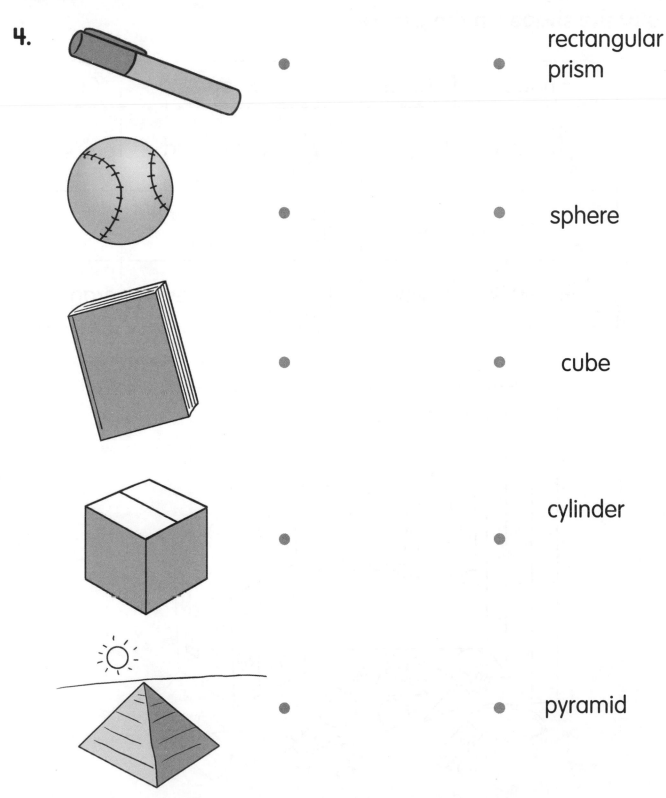

rectangular prism

sphere

cube

cylinder

pyramid

Look at the picture.
Color the shapes in the picture.

5.

Shape		Color
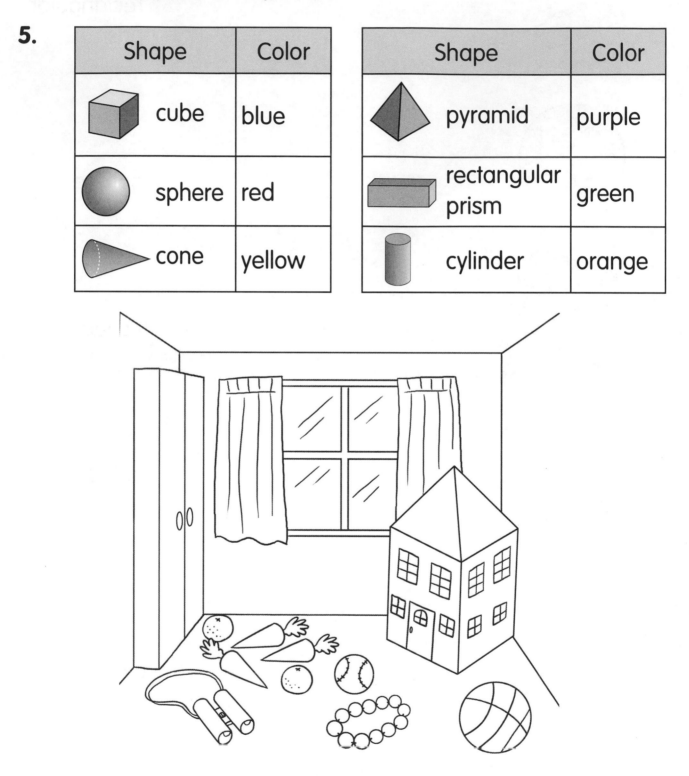 cube		blue
sphere		red
cone		yellow

Shape		Color
pyramid		purple
rectangular prism		green
cylinder		orange

What shape is <u>not</u> in the picture? _____

Practice 7   Making Patterns with Plane Shapes

Sort the shapes.
Write the numbers in the correct boxes.

1.

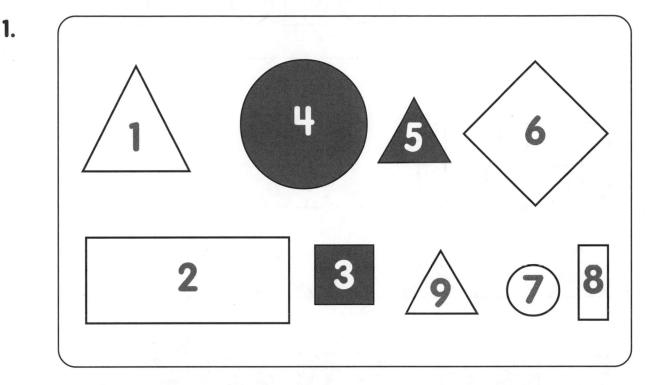

Shape

Circles	Triangles	Squares	Rectangles
4 7			

Size

Big	Small

Color

Black	White

Complete the patterns.
Draw the missing shape.

Example

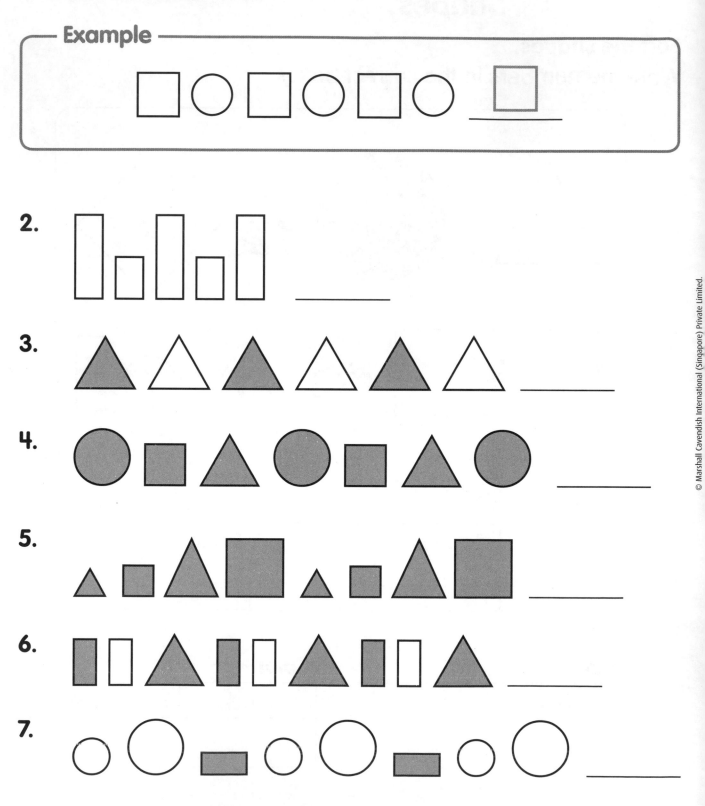

2.

3.

4.

5.

6.

7.

Complete the patterns.
Circle the missing shape.

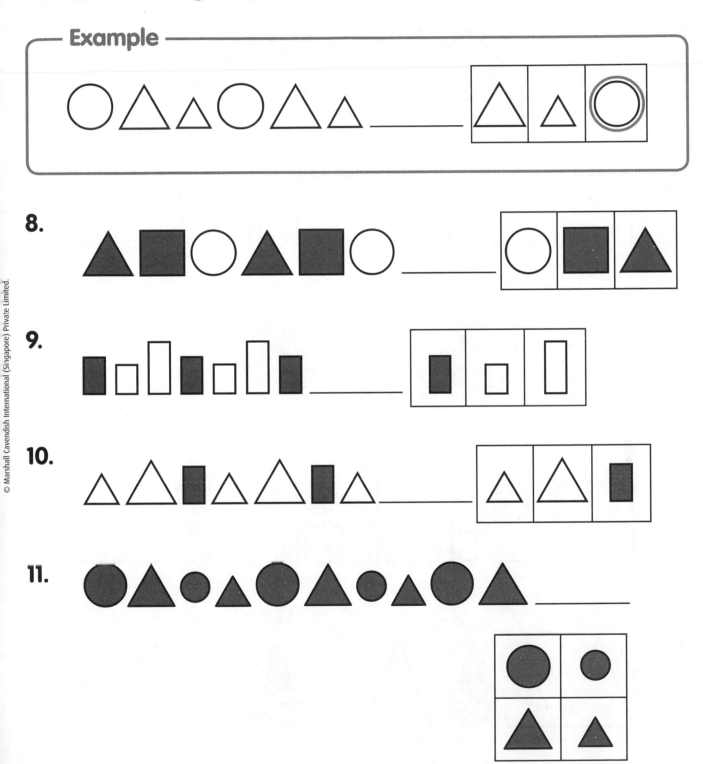

Complete the patterns.
Draw what comes next.

12. _____

13. _____

14. _____

15. _____

16. _____

Cut out the shapes below.
Make two patterns.
You do not need to use all the shapes.

17. Paste your first pattern here.

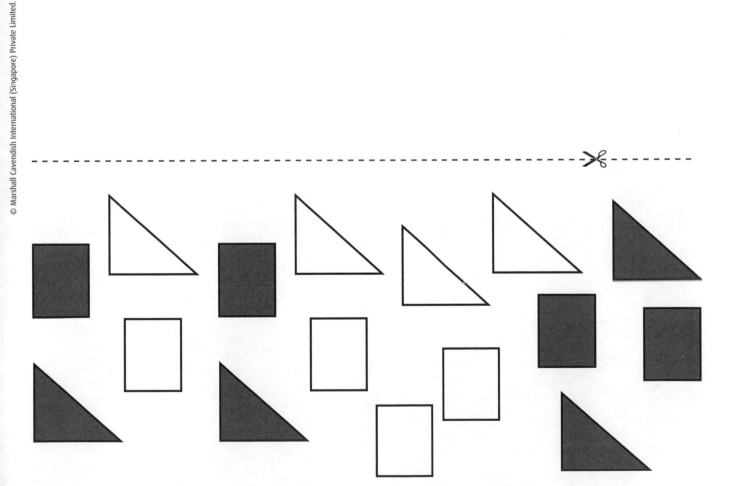

18. Paste your second pattern here.

- ✂ - - - - - - - - -

Practice 8   Making Patterns with Solid Shapes

Complete the patterns.
Circle the shape that comes next.

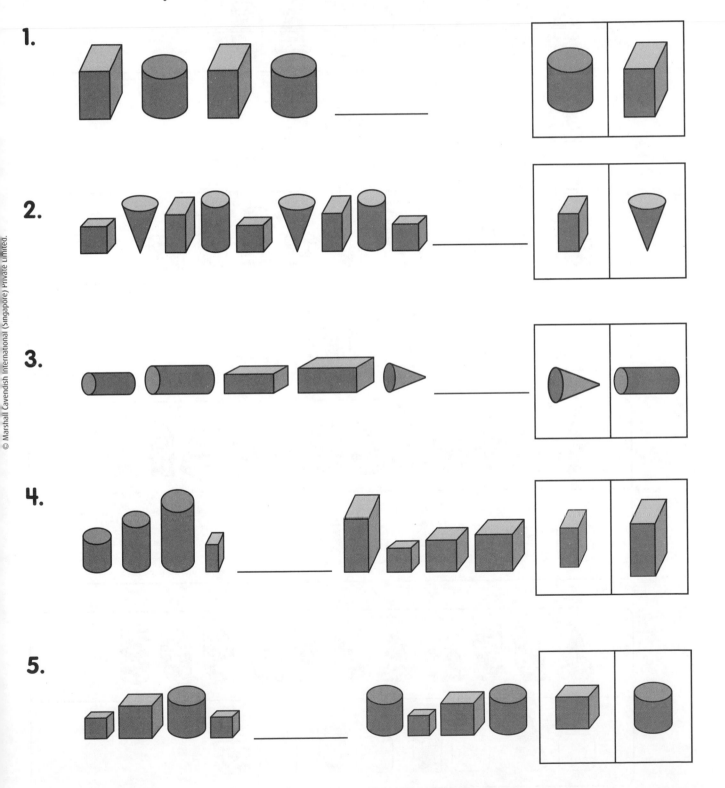

1.

2.

3.

4.

5.

Circle the mistake in the pattern.
Then make a ✔ for the correct shape.

Example

6.

7.

8.

Name: _____ **Date:** _____

Math Journal

Choose two things.
Circle them.

1.

jar   sharpener   brick   ice-cream cone

Now write about them.
Use the words in the box to help you.

cylinder   sphere   cube   cone   pyramid   rectangular prism

stacking   sliding   rolling   size   shape

2. The _____ has the shape of a _____.

3. The _____ has the shape of a _____.

4. I can move the _____ by _____.

5. I can move the _____ by _____.

Continued on next page

6. My things are alike because they _____

_____.

7. My things are different because they _____

_____.

Make a pattern with plane shapes.
Read and draw.

8. The shapes in this pattern are alike.
The sizes of the shapes are different.

Put On Your Thinking Cap!

Challenging Practice

Solve.

1. Lee, Jen, Bob, and Dean have some shapes.
   Find out who has each set of shapes.

   - Lee has fewer circles than Bob.

   - All of Jen's shapes have 3 sides or more.

   - Bob has four kinds of shapes.

   - Dean has no squares.

   Write the name that matches each set on the line below.

_____   _____

_____   _____

Cut out the pieces of shapes on page 135.
Paste the cut-out pieces to fit the two pictures below.

2.

3.

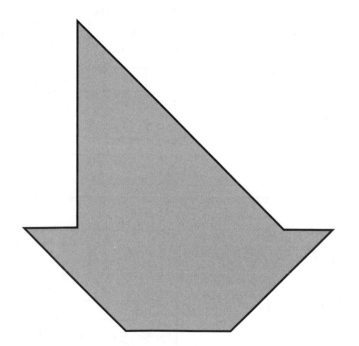

Name: _____ **Date:** _____

2.

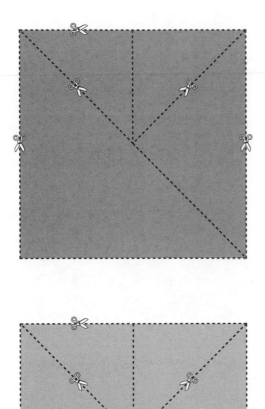

3.

Name: _____   Date: _____

Put On Your Thinking Cap!
Problem Solving

Draw and complete the pattern.
Each row (↔) and column (↕) must have these four
shapes, ○ △ □ ▭.

1.

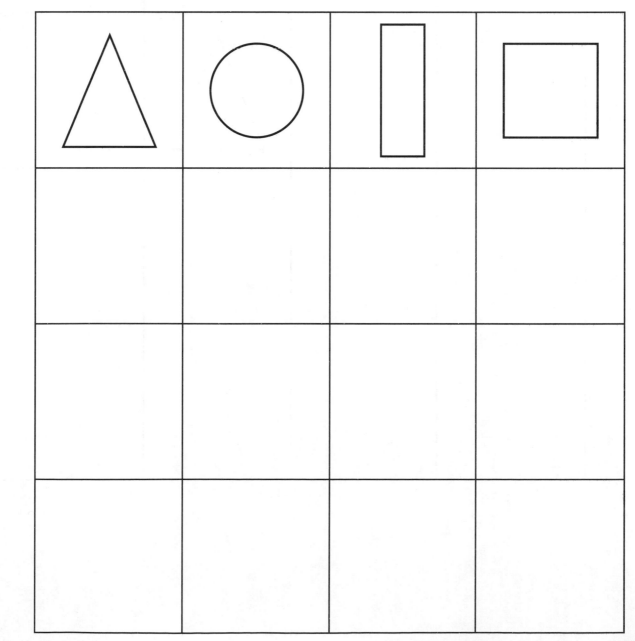

Draw and complete the pattern.
Each row (↔) and column (↕) must have these four shapes,
◯□□△.

2.

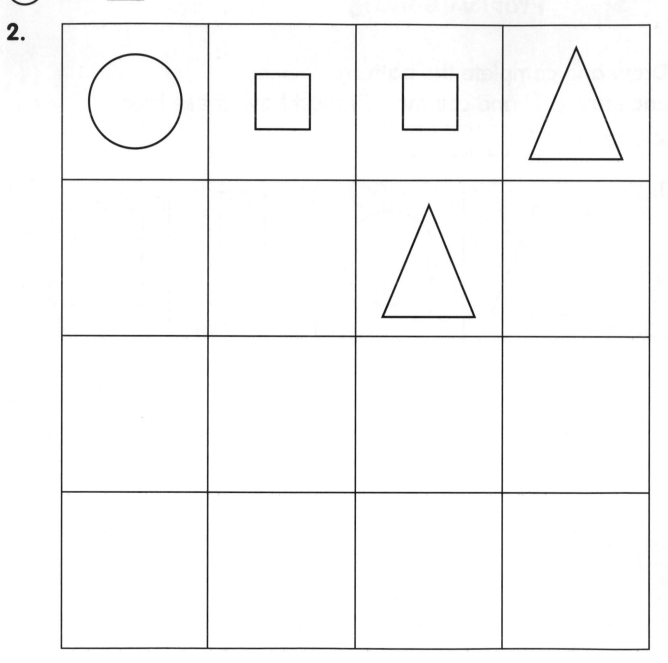

Chapter Review/Test

Vocabulary

Draw the shape.

1. square   **2.** rectangle   **3.** triangle

Write the name.
Use the words in the box.

4.   **5.**

cylinder
——————
sphere

_____   _____

Concepts and Skills

Trace the shape.
Write the number of sides and corners.

6.

_____ sides

_____ corners

7.

_____ sides

_____ corners

Circle the correct answer.

8. The square is made up of two / four equal parts.

9. One half of / fourth of the square is shaded.

Answer the question.
Write *yes* or *no*.

10. How are these shapes alike?

a. same shape _____   b. same size _____

c. same color _____

Circle the solid shapes you can roll.

11.

Name: _____ **Date:** _____

How can you move a pyramid?
Circle the answer.

12.

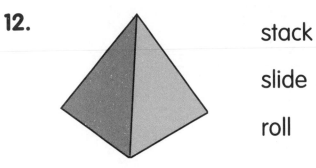

stack

slide

roll

Look at the picture.
What shapes do you see?
Circle the answers.

13.

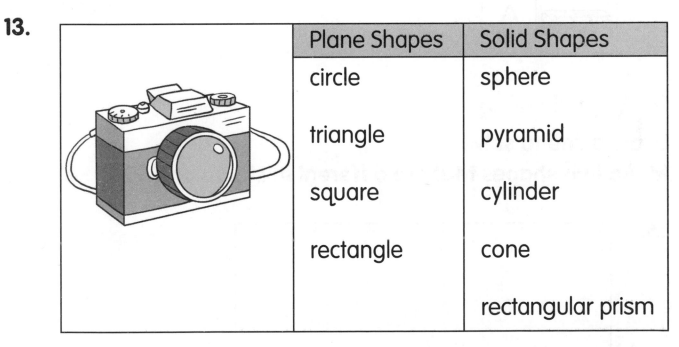

Plane Shapes	Solid Shapes
circle	sphere
triangle	pyramid
square	cylinder
rectangle	cone
	rectangular prism

Complete the pattern.
Circle the shape that comes next.

14.

15.

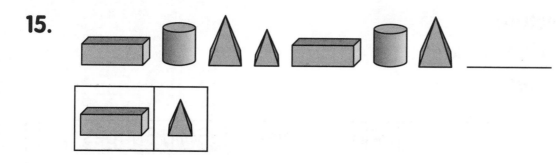

Problem Solving

Draw a line to solve.
Make two shapes that are different in shape and size.

16.

CHAPTER 6 Ordinal Numbers and Position

Practice 1 Ordinal Numbers

Circle.

Example

the 2nd corn

1. the 5th princess

2. the 8th bird

3. the 7th duckling

Color.

4. 3 frogs

the 3rd frog

5. 10 ants

the 10th ant

Name: _____   Date: _____

Match.

first   •

second   •

third   •

fourth   •

fifth   •

sixth   •

seventh   •

eighth   •

ninth   •

tenth   •

Look at the picture.
Answer the questions.

7. Who is first in the race? _____

8. Who is fourth in the race? _____

9. In which position is Tandi? _____

10. In which position is Jenn? _____

11. Who is last? _____

Practice 2   Position Words

Look at the picture.
Circle the correct name.

Eddie   Denelle   Carlo   Ben   Alice

Example

Who is after Alice?   Carlo   (Ben)

---

1. Who is before Ben?   Carlo   Alice

2. Who is after Carlo?   Ben   Denelle

3. Who is between Eddie and Carlo?   Alice   Denelle

4. Who is between Carlo and Alice?   Ben   Eddie

Color.

the fourth bird from the left

5. the second pizza from the left

6. the fifth monkey from the right

7. the ninth football from the right

Name: _____ Date: _____

Look at the picture.
Fill in the blanks with the words in the box.

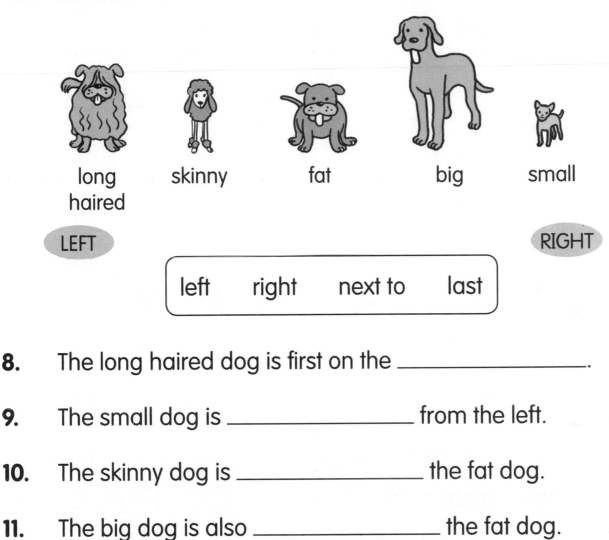

long haired   skinny   fat   big   small

LEFT   RIGHT

left	right	next to	last

8. The long haired dog is first on the _____.

9. The small dog is _____ from the left.

10. The skinny dog is _____ the fat dog.

11. The big dog is also _____ the fat dog.

Draw.

12. an apple on the last plate from the right
a banana on the plate next to the apple
an orange on the sixth plate from the left

Read the clues to answer the question.
Then write the letters in the correct ☐ **.**

13. What is the capital of the United States of America?

☐ ☐ ☐ ☐ ☐ ☐ ☐ ☐ ☐ ☐ D.C.
a   b   c   d   e   f   g   h   i   j

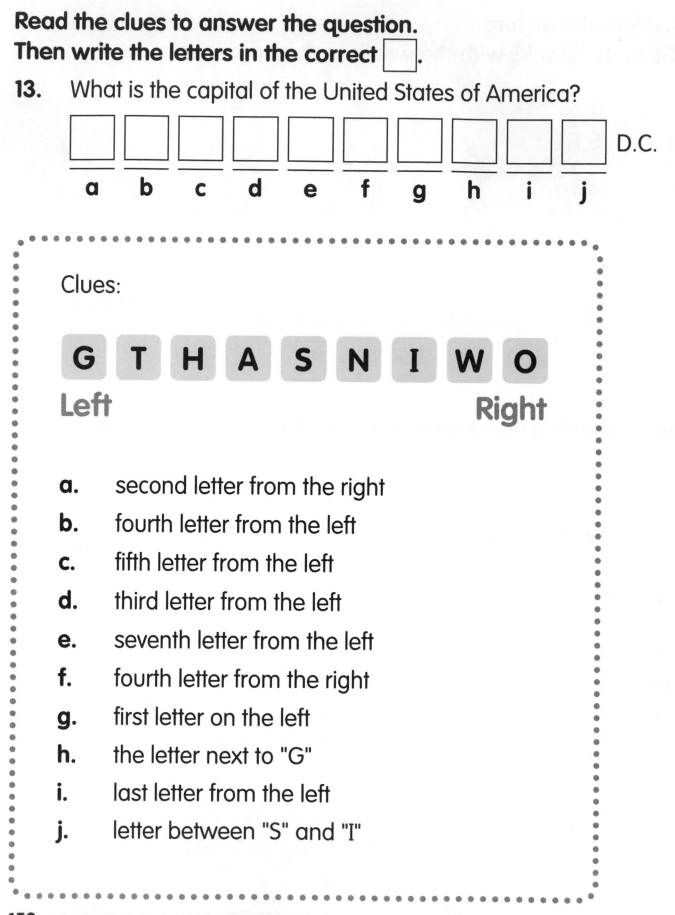

Clues:

G T H A S N I W O
Left   Right

a. second letter from the right

b. fourth letter from the left

c. fifth letter from the left

d. third letter from the left

e. seventh letter from the left

f. fourth letter from the right

g. first letter on the left

h. the letter next to "G"

i. last letter from the left

j. letter between "S" and "I"

Practice 3   Position Words

Color.

1.   the rabbit below the black rabbit pink
        the rabbit above the black rabbit gray
        the rabbit under the paper brown
        the hair of the boy behind the shelf yellow
        the hair of the boy in front of the shelf red

Look at the picture.
Fill in the blanks with the words in the box.

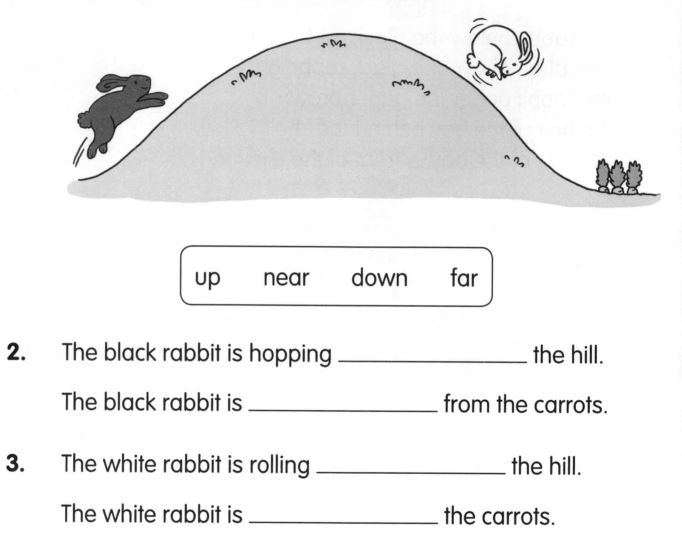

| up | near | down | far |

2. The black rabbit is hopping _____ the hill.

    The black rabbit is _____ from the carrots.

3. The white rabbit is rolling _____ the hill.

    The white rabbit is _____ the carrots.

Put On Your Thinking Cap!

Challenging Practice

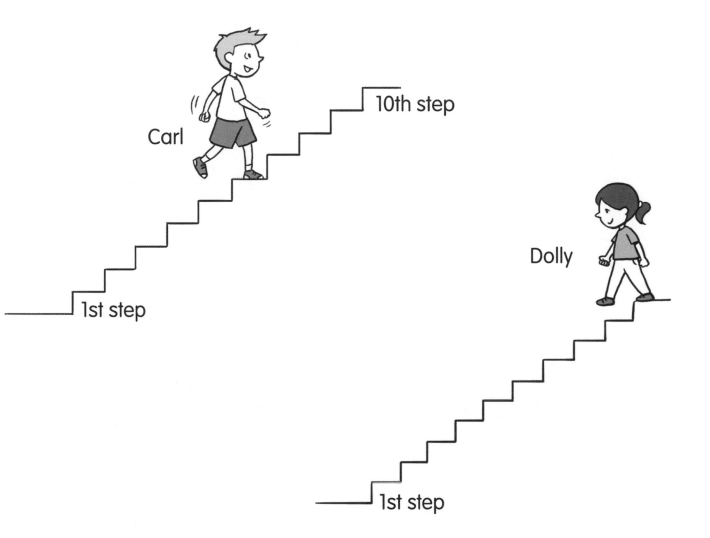

1. When Carl climbs up four steps, he will be on the tenth step.

   Carl is on the _____ step now.

2. When Dolly walks down three steps, she will be on the seventh step.

   Dolly is on the _____ step now.

Put On Your Thinking Cap!

Problem Solving

1. There are four rabbits, A, B, C, and D.
   Read the clues.
   Fill in the circles with the correct letters.

Rabbit A is 4th from the right.

Rabbit C is next to Rabbit A.

Rabbit D is between Rabbit C and Rabbit B.

2. Look at the pictures.
Put them in order.
Write the ordinal number that belongs with each picture.

7th	4th	6th	2nd	1st
8th	3rd	9th	5th	10th

3. Michael has some cards in these shapes.

He makes this pattern:

Continue the pattern.
What is the shape of the tenth card from the left?

Draw to find out.

The tenth card from the left is [   ] .

Chapter Review/Test

Vocabulary

Match.

1. 7th   •   • ninth

    3rd   •   • fifth

    5th   •   • seventh

    10th   •   • third

    9th   •   • tenth

**Look at the chipmunks.
Where is the acorn?
Circle the correct word.**

2.

left   right

3.

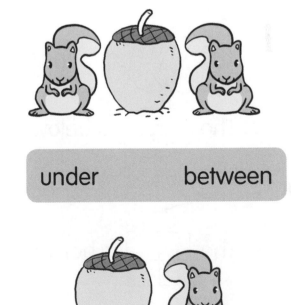

under   between

4.

next to   behind

5.

in front of   next to

Concepts and Skills

Read and draw.

6. The are under the bed.

7. The is below the picture.

8. The is far from the cat.

9. The is between the clock and the picture.

10. The is above the bed.

11. The is in front of the cat.

Name: _____   **Date:** _____

Look at the picture.
Fill in the blanks.

Gina

Ella

Ryan

Brad

up	after	before	down	between

12. Ryan is climbing _____ the steps.

13. Gina, Ella, and Brad are sliding _____ the slide.

14. Gina is _____ Ella.

15. Brad is _____ Ella.

16. Ella is _____ Brad and Gina.

Problem Solving

Color.

17.

LEFT   RIGHT

The first ball on the right is blue.

The last ball from the right is orange.

The ball next to the blue ball is red.

The ball between the orange and red ball is green.

The balloon above the shelf is yellow.

The balloon below the shelf is black.

Name: _____ **Date:** _____

Cumulative Review

for Chapters 5 and 6

Concepts and Skills

Look at the picture.
Count and write the number of shapes you see.

1.

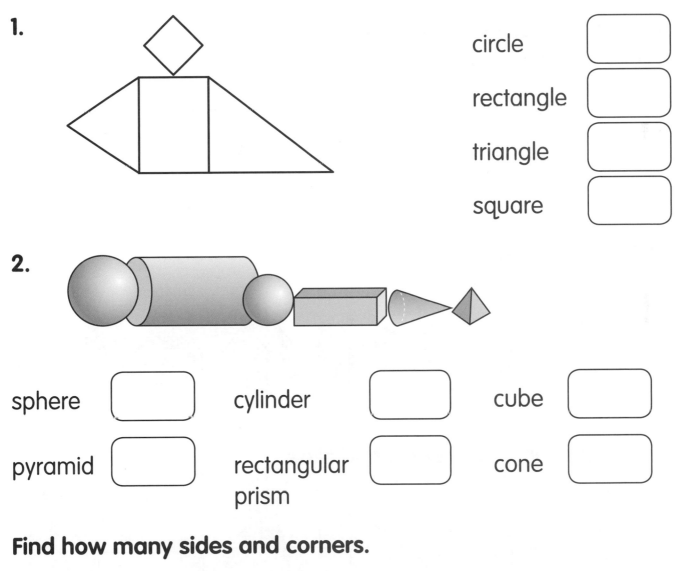

circle ▢

rectangle ▢

triangle ▢

square ▢

2.

sphere ▢   cylinder ▢   cube ▢

pyramid ▢   rectangular prism ▢   cone ▢

Find how many sides and corners.

3.

_____ sides

_____ corners

Sort the shapes by <u>size.</u>
Color the shapes that are <u>different.</u>

4.

Sort the shapes by the <u>number of sides.</u>
Color the shapes that are <u>alike.</u>

5.

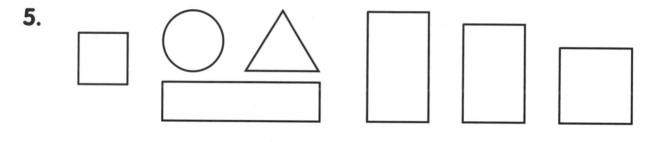

Circle the shapes that roll.

6.

Circle the shapes that stack <u>and</u> slide.

7.

Name: _____   **Date:** _____

Look at the picture.
Circle the correct answer.

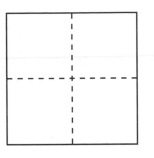

8.   How many equal parts make up the square?   2   4

9.   Color two parts of the square blue.

10.   Two   (halves / quarters)   are blue.

Complete the pattern.
Circle the missing shape.

11.

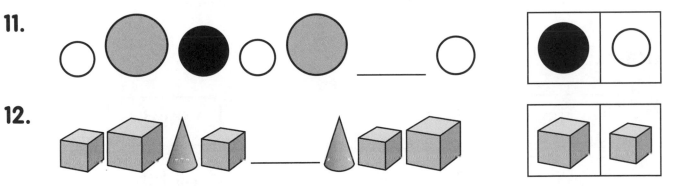

12.

Color.

13. the 3rd sticker

1st

14. the 6th baseball glove

3rd

15. the 10th ladybug

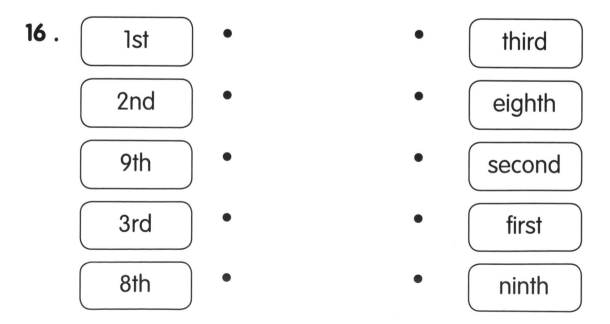

4th

Match.

16 .

1st	•	•	third
2nd	•	•	eighth
9th	•	•	second
3rd	•	•	first
8th	•	•	ninth

Name: _____   Date: _____

Look at each picture.
Circle the correct word.

17. Andy is (after / before) Eva.

18. Emma is (before / between) Tandi and Mark.

19. Tandi is (after / between) Emma and Mark.

20. Mark is 2nd from the (left / right).

21. Andy is (first / last) on the left.

22. Mark is (in front of / behind) Tandi.

23. Andy is (near / far from) Eva.

Problem Solving

Solve.

24. Shantel draws a rectangle.
Then she draws a line to make two new shapes.
The two new shapes are alike.
Each new shape is the same shape and size.
Each new shape has 3 corners and 3 sides.

Draw a line to make the two shapes.

Complete.

25. This is a shape pattern.

a. Color the 3rd shape.

b. Draw the next three shapes in the pattern.

c. Draw the 9th shape.

d. The 1st shape is a square.
The 4th shape is a square.

The _____ shape is also a square.

CHAPTER 7 Numbers to 20

Practice 1   Counting to 20

Write the numbers.

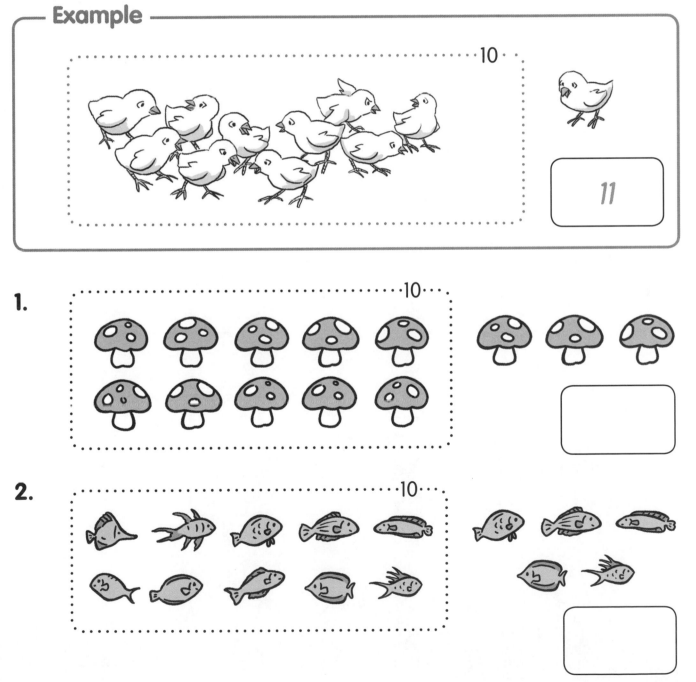

Example

10

11

1.   10

2.   10

3.

···10···

4.

···10···

Circle the ten.
Color the rest.
Write the numbers.

┌─ **Example** ──────────────────────────────────┐

12

└──┘

5.

_____

6.

_____

7.

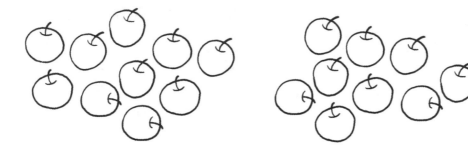

_____

Fill in the blanks.

8.

10 and 3 make _____.

10 + 3 = _____

9.

10 and 6 make _____.

10 + 6 = _____

10.

10 and 9 make _____.

10 + 9 = _____

11.

10 and 8 make _____.

10 + 8 = _____

Fill in the blanks with the correct number or word.

12. _____ and _____ make 12.

13. _____ and _____ make 15.

14. _____ is ten and four.

15. _____ is seven and ten.

Name: _____ Date: _____

Fill in the blanks.

16.   10 + 3 = _____   **17.**   10 + 4 = _____

18.   10 + 5 = _____   **19.**   10 + 6 = _____

20.   10 + 9 = _____   **21.**   10 + 10 = _____

22.   2 + 10 = _____   **23.**   8 + 10 = _____

Count.
Circle the correct word.

— Example —

10

seven

(eleven)

24.

10

twelve

two

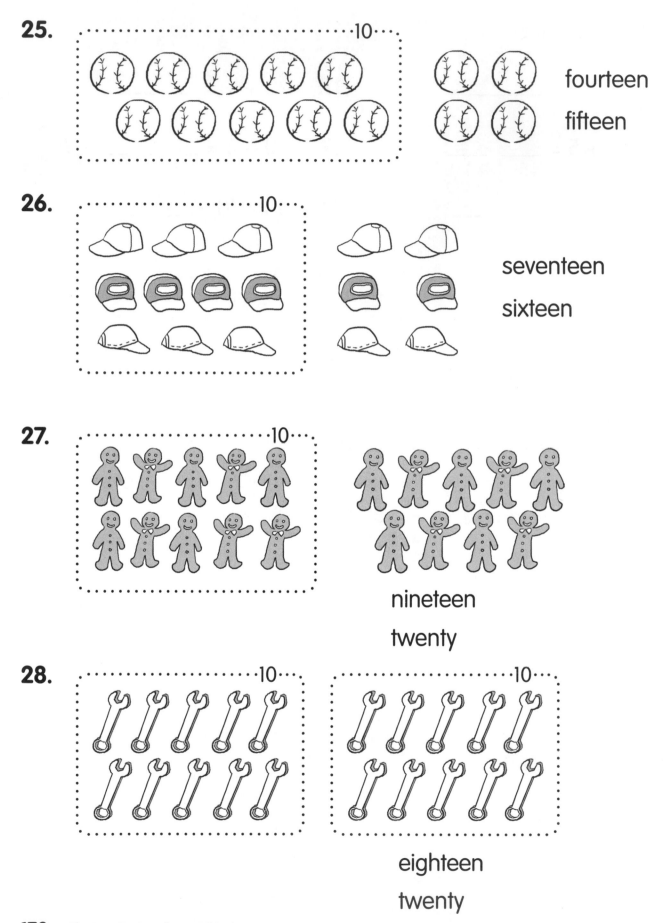

25.

10

fourteen

fifteen

26.

10

seventeen

sixteen

27.

10

nineteen

twenty

28.

10   10

eighteen

twenty

Practice 2 Place Value

Look at the pictures.
Fill in the blanks.

┌─ **Example** ─────────────────────────────────┐
│
│ ········10·······
│
│ ___*1*___ ten ___*3*___ ones
│
└───┘

1.

········10·······

_____ ten _____ ones

2.

········10·······

_____ ten _____ ones

3.

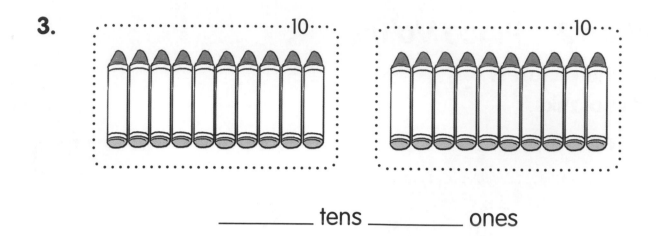

_____ tens _____ ones

Fill in the place-value charts.

Example

	Tens	Ones
19	1	9

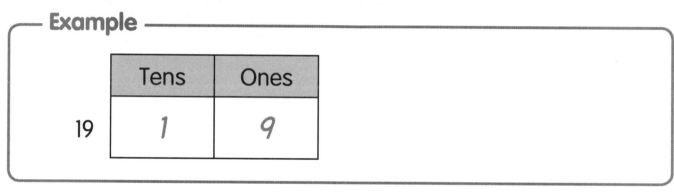

4.

	Tens	Ones
11		

5.

	Tens	Ones
12		

6.

	Tens	Ones
15		

7.

	Tens	Ones
20		

Show the number.

Draw ▯ for tens and ☐ for ones.

┌─ **Example** ──────────────────────────────────┐

Tens	Ones
13	

In the table: under Tens column there is ▯, under Ones column there are ☐ ☐ ☐

└──┘

8.

Tens	Ones

12

9.

Tens	Ones

16

10.

Tens	Ones

18

11.

Tens	Ones

19

Look at the place-value charts.
Write the numbers.

12.

Tens	Ones

_____

13.

Tens	Ones

_____

14.

Tens	Ones

_____

15.

Tens	Ones

_____

Fill in the blanks.

16.   13 = 1 ten _____ ones

17.   17 = _____ ten 7 ones

18.   15 = 1 ten _____ ones

19.   12 = _____ ten 2 ones

20.   19 = 1 ten _____ ones

Practice 3   Comparing Numbers

Write the number in each set.
Then fill in the blanks.

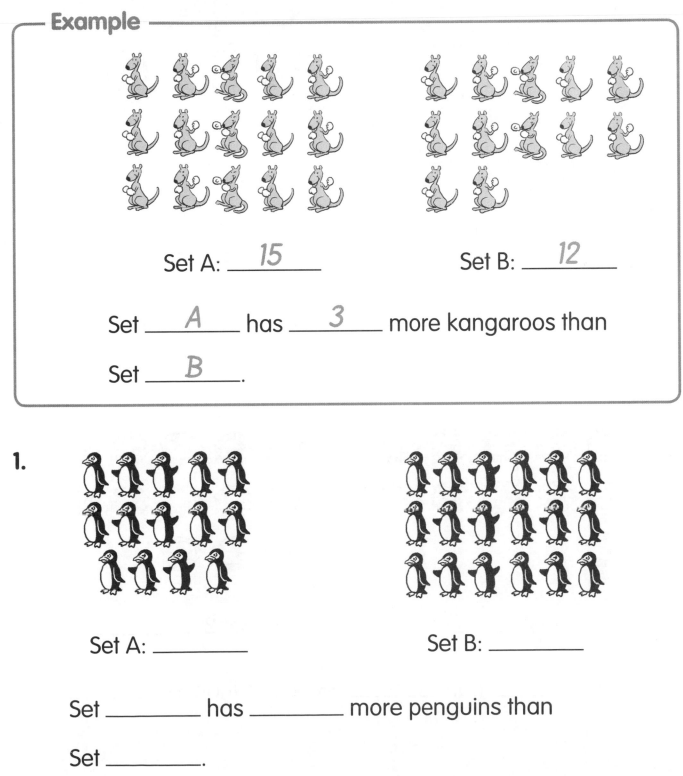

┌─ **Example** ─────────────────────────────────

Set A: _____15_____   Set B: _____12_____

Set _____A_____ has _____3_____ more kangaroos than

Set _____B_____.

───┘

1.

Set A: _____   Set B: _____

Set _____ has _____ more penguins than

Set _____.

Write the number in each set.
Then fill in the blanks.

2.

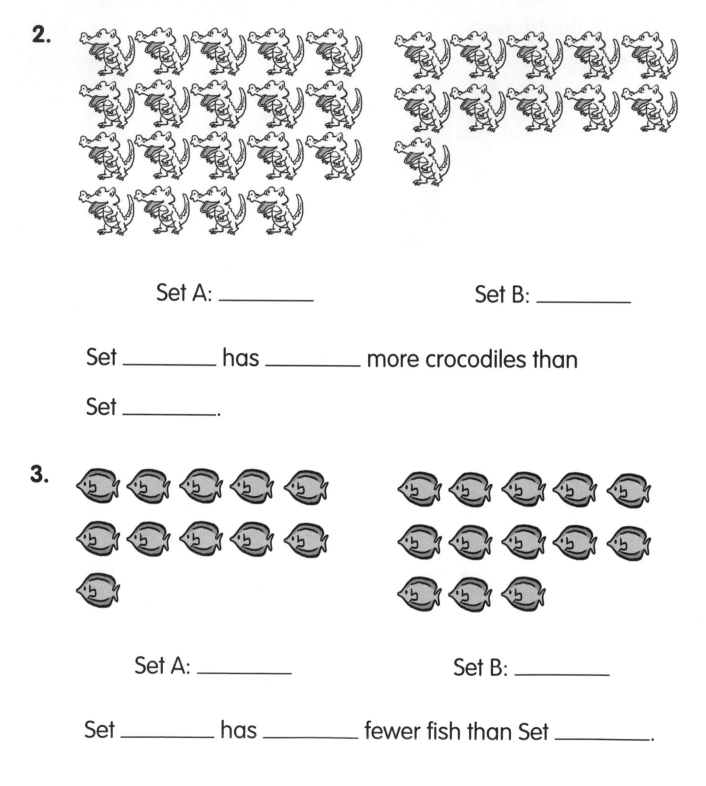

Set A: _____   Set B: _____

Set _____ has _____ more crocodiles than

Set _____.

3.

Set A: _____   Set B: _____

Set _____ has _____ fewer fish than Set _____.

4.

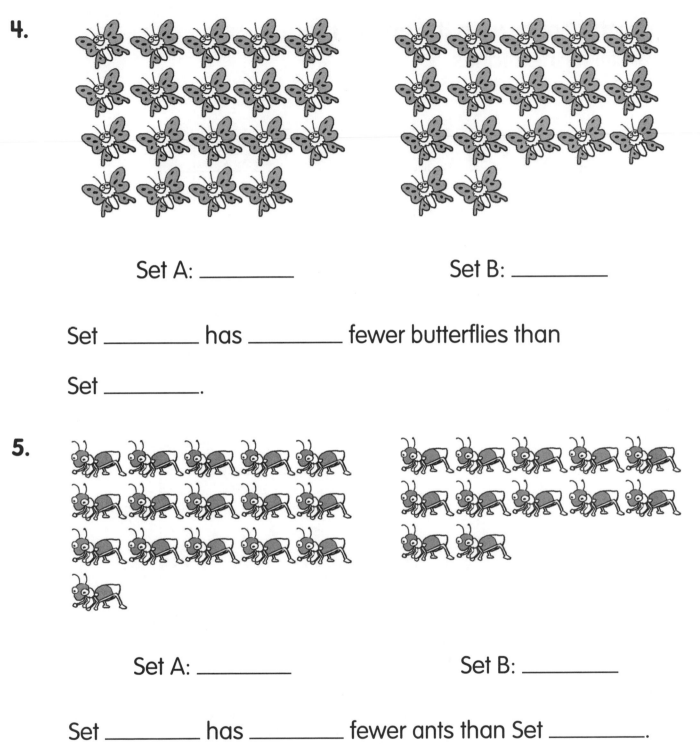

Set A: _____   Set B: _____

Set _____ has _____ fewer butterflies than

Set _____.

5.

Set A: _____   Set B: _____

Set _____ has _____ fewer ants than Set _____.

© Marshall Cavendish International (Singapore) Private Limited.

Color the house with the number that is less.
Then fill in the blanks.

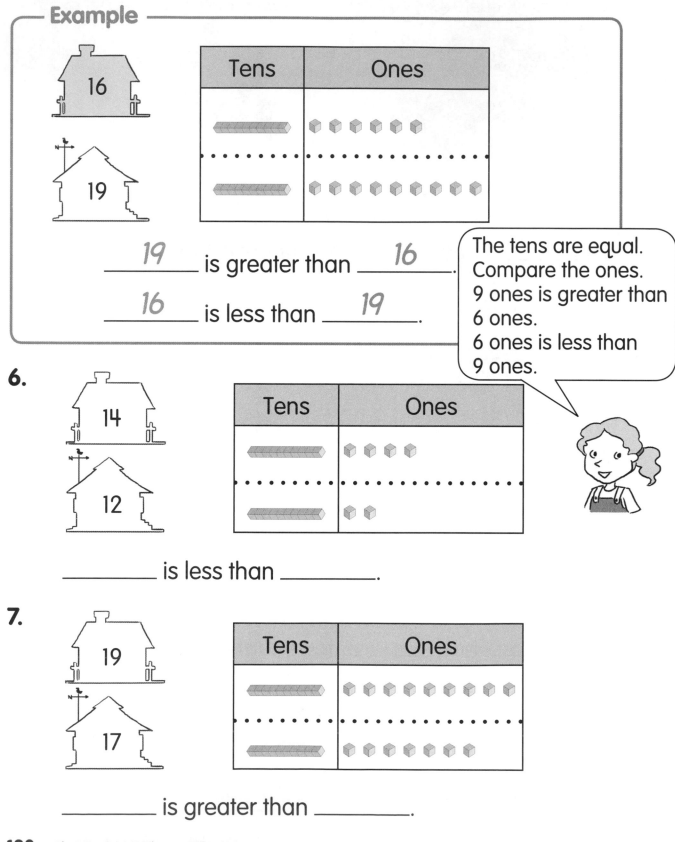

Example

Tens	Ones

_____*19*_____ is greater than _____*16*_____.
_____*16*_____ is less than _____*19*_____.

The tens are equal.
Compare the ones.
9 ones is greater than
6 ones.
6 ones is less than
9 ones.

6.

Tens	Ones

_____ is less than _____.

7.

Tens	Ones

_____ is greater than _____.

Find the number that is less.
Color the animal red.
Find the number that is greater.
Color the animal blue.

8.

9.

Color the creature with the correct number.
Then fill in the blanks.

10.   the number that is greater

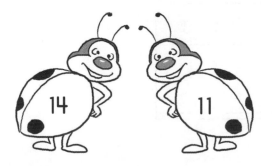

How much greater is the number? _____

11. the number that is less

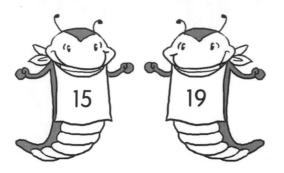

How much less is the number? _____

Fill in the blanks in each place-value chart.
Then color the sign with the greatest number.

12.

Tens	Ones
_1_	_9_

Tens	Ones

Tens	Ones

Name: _____ **Date:** _____

Fill in the blanks in each place-value chart.
Then color the sign with the least number.

13.

Tens	Ones
____	____

Tens	Ones
____	____

Tens	Ones
____	____

Compare the numbers.
Fill in the blanks.

14.

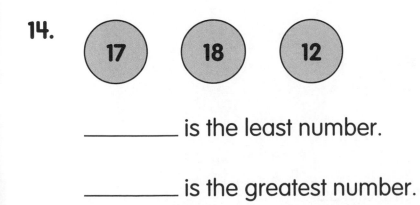

_____ is the least number.

_____ is the greatest number.

Compare the numbers.
Fill in the blanks.

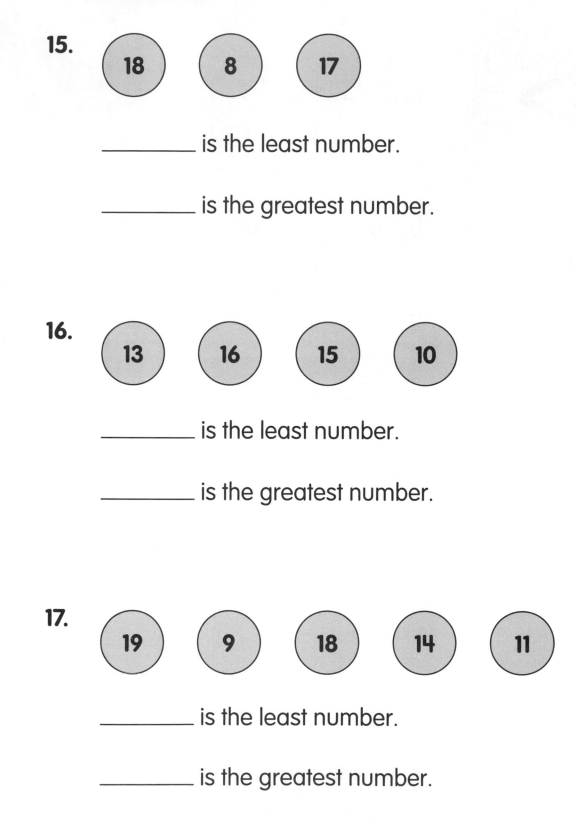

15.

18   8   17

_____ is the least number.

_____ is the greatest number.

16.

13   16   15   10

_____ is the least number.

_____ is the greatest number.

17.

19   9   18   14   11

_____ is the least number.

_____ is the greatest number.

Practice 4   Making Patterns and Ordering Numbers

Solve.

1. Alex uses circles to make a pattern.
   How many circles come next in the pattern?
   Draw the circles in the empty box.
   Write the number of circles below this box.

_____

Complete the patterns.

2.

3.

Look at the numbers.
Fill in the blanks.

20   17   18   19   15

4.   _____ is 2 more than 15.

5.   _____ is 2 less than 20.

6.   1 more than 18 is _____.

7.   2 less than 19 is _____.

Complete the number patterns.

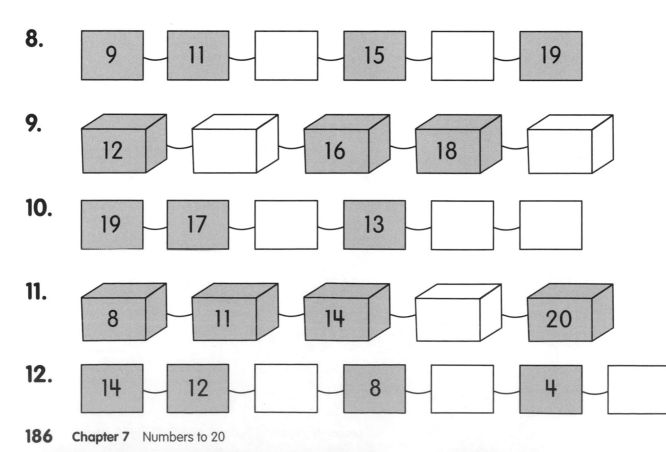

8.   9 | 11 | | 15 | | 19

9.   12 | | 16 | 18 |

10.   19 | 17 | | 13 | |

11.   8 | 11 | 14 | | 20

12.   14 | 12 | | 8 | | 4 |

Name: _____   **Date:** _____

Help Rosa order the bowling pins and balls.

13. Write the numbers on the in order from least to greatest.

12

least

14. Write the numbers on the 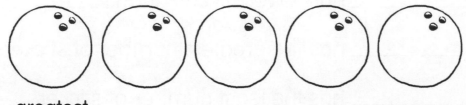 in order from greatest to least.

greatest

Math Journal

Count how many stickers the boys have.
Fill in the blanks.

1.

Pete has _____ stickers.   Ty has _____ stickers.

Draw how many stickers you have.
Then fill in the blanks.

2.

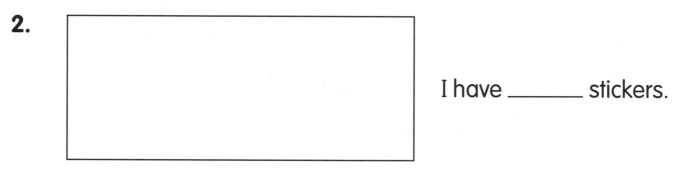

I have _____ stickers.

Write about the number of stickers everyone has.
Fill in the blanks with the correct names.

3. _____ has more stickers than _____.

4. _____ has fewer stickers than _____.

5. _____ has the greatest number of stickers.

6. _____ has the least number of stickers.

Put On Your Thinking Cap!

Challenging Practice

1. Class 1A of Greenfield School holds a basketball contest.
Find out who won.

CLUES

Rita scores the least number of baskets.

John scores 3 more baskets than Rita.

Dion scores more baskets than Rachel but less than Frank.

Write the names next to the number of baskets scored.

Baskets Scored

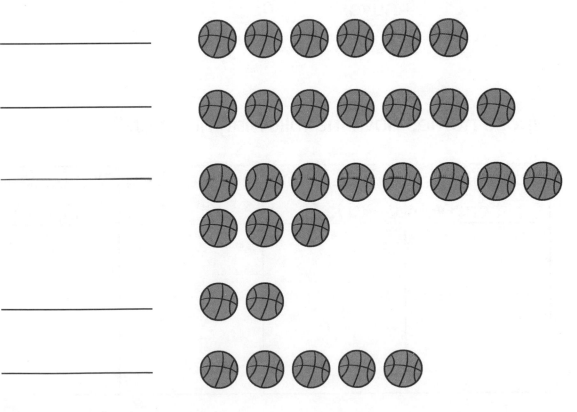

Who won the contest? _____

Fill in the blanks.

2.   10 + _____ = 15

3.   10 + _____ = 11

4.   10 + _____ = 18

5.   _____ + 10 = 14

6.   _____ + 10 = 17

Write the correct names.

7.   These are the numbers of 12 players on a team.

Whose names have the following numbers?

Numbers less than 5	Numbers from 5 to 9	Numbers from 10 to 14	Numbers from 15 to 20

Put On Your Thinking Cap!

Problem Solving

Use the clues on the next page.
Help Tony find which numbers his counters covered.

Read what Tony's friends said.

Circle the numbers that were covered on Tony's card.

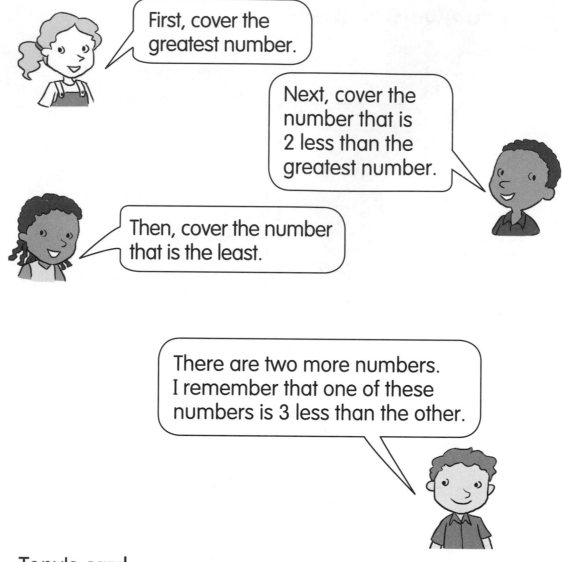

First, cover the greatest number.

Next, cover the number that is 2 less than the greatest number.

Then, cover the number that is the least.

There are two more numbers. I remember that one of these numbers is 3 less than the other.

Tony's card.

1	9	13	18
5	3	7	17
16	11	15	12

Chapter Review/Test

Vocabulary

Unscramble the letters to spell each number.

1. 15 f i e e t f n

   _____

2. 11 e v l e e n

   _____

3. 18 e g e e t h n i

   _____

4. 20 t w y n e t

   _____

Fill in the blank with the correct word.

> place-value chart   compare

5. You can show numbers as tens and ones in

   a _____.

6. When you _____ 12 and 15, 12 is the number that is less.

Concepts and Skills

Count. Write the number.

7.

_____ puppets

© Marshall Cavendish International (Singapore) Private Limited.

8.

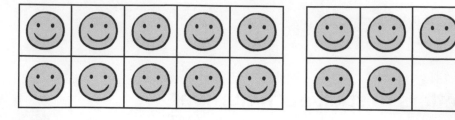

_____ faces.

Fill in the blanks.

9.

Set A: _____   Set B: _____

Set _____ has _____ more oranges than Set _____.

Set _____ has _____ fewer oranges than Set _____.

Which is the greater number? _____

Complete the number pattern.

10.   13, 14, _____, _____, 17, _____, 19

11.   19, 17, _____, 13, 11, _____

Write the numbers in order from least to greatest.

12.

| 17 | 3 | 0 | 10 | 15 |

_____ , _____ , _____ , _____ , _____

Write the numbers in order from greatest to least.

13.

| 11 | 19 | 8 | 9 | 14 |

_____ , _____ , _____ , _____ , _____

Problem Solving

Read the clues.

Then cross out the numbers to solve.

Example

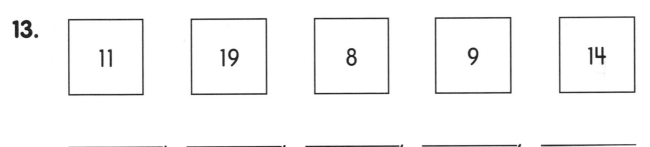

I am greater than 13.
I am less than 17.
Of the numbers that are left:
   I am not the least.
   I am not the greatest.
What number am I? _____*15*_____

14.

| 10 | 11 | 12 | 13 | 14 | 15 | 16 | 17 | 18 | 19 | 20 |

I am less than 20.
I am more than 13.
I am less than 17.
I am 4 more than 12.
What number am I? _____

15.

| 10 | 11 | 12 | 13 | 14 | 15 | 16 | 17 | 18 | 19 | 20 |

a.   I am more than 10.
I am less than 20.
I am more than 12.
I am less than 15.
Of the numbers that are left:
I am the greater number.
What number am I? _____

b.   Draw the number in the place-value chart.
Draw ▯ for tens and □ for ones.

Tens	Ones

Addition and Subtraction Facts to 20

Practice 1   Ways to Add

Make a 10.
Then add.

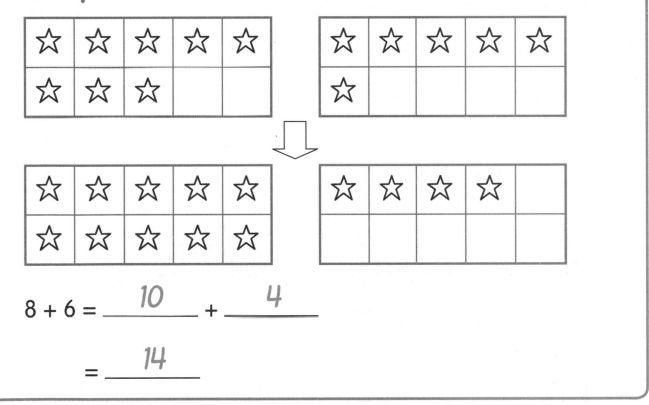

Example

$$8 + 6 = \underline{\quad 10 \quad} + \underline{\quad 4 \quad}$$

$$= \underline{\quad 14 \quad}$$

1.

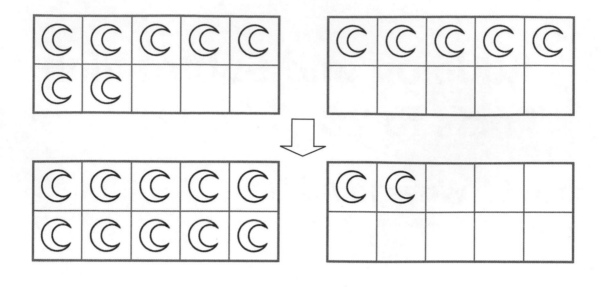

$7 + 5 =$ _____ + _____

$=$ _____

2.

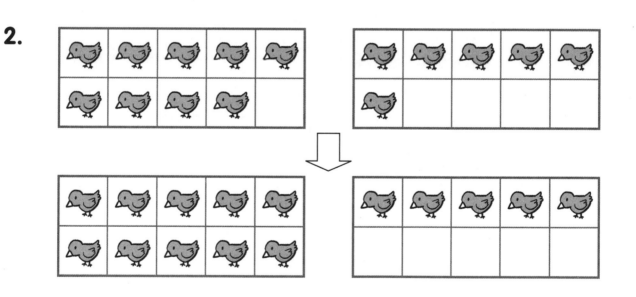

$9 + 6 =$ _____ + _____

$=$ _____

Draw 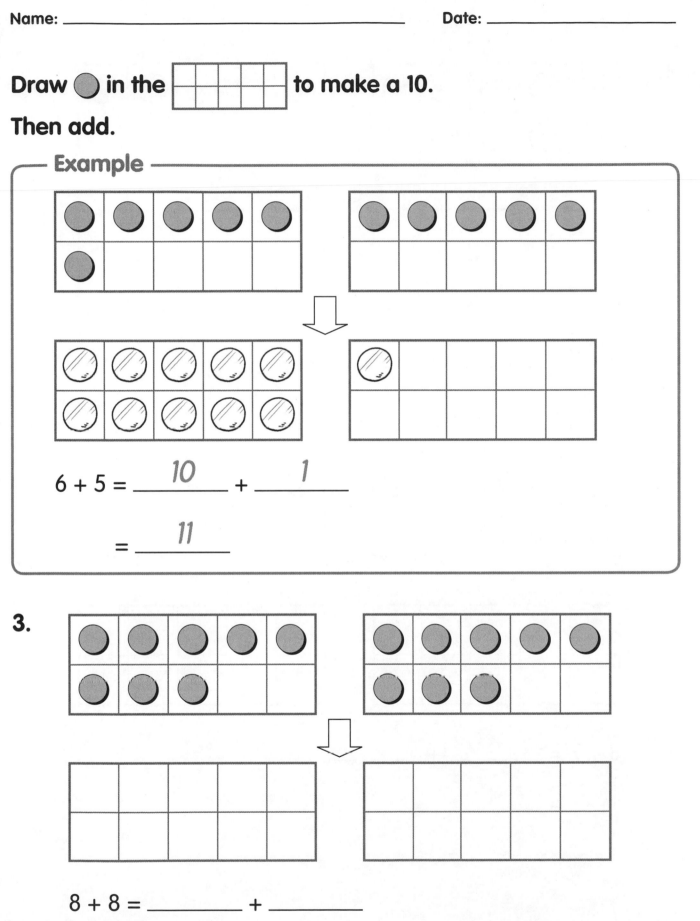 in the ⬚⬚⬚⬚⬚ to make a 10.

Then add.

Example

$6 + 5 =$ ___10___ $+$ ___1___

$=$ ___11___

3.

$8 + 8 =$ _____ $+$ _____

$=$ _____

4.

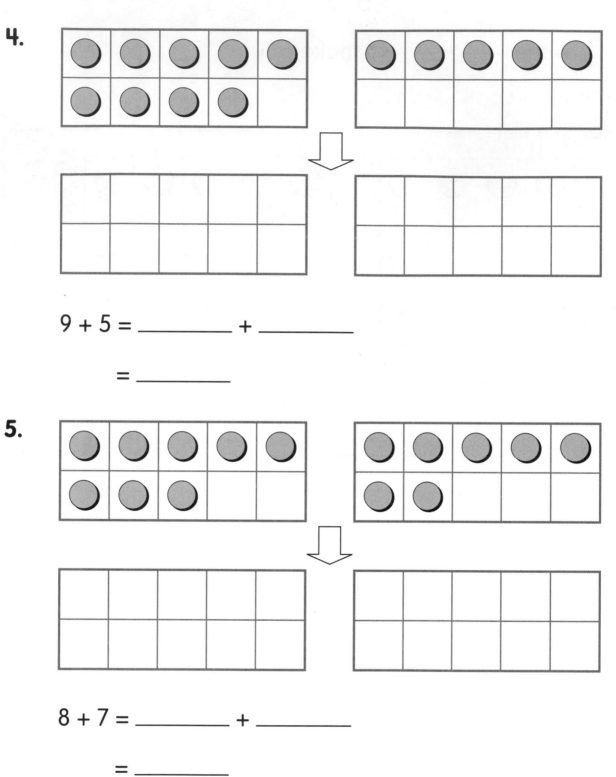

$9 + 5 =$ _____ $+$ _____

$=$ _____

5.

$8 + 7 =$ _____ $+$ _____

$=$ _____

Draw ⬤ in the ⬚⬚ to show the numbers.

Then draw ⬤ in the ⬚⬚ and add.

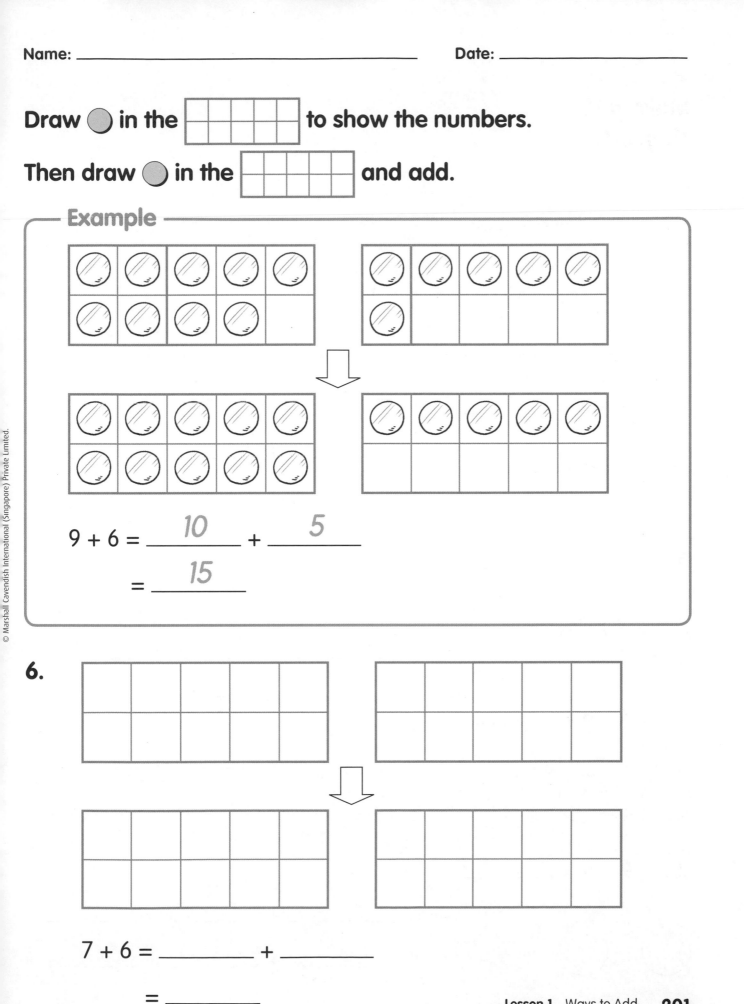

Example

$9 + 6 =$ ___10___ $+$ ___5___

$=$ ___15___

6.

$7 + 6 =$ _____ $+$ _____

$=$ _____

Make a 10.
Then add.

Example

$3 + 8 = \underline{\quad 11 \quad}$

$\underline{\quad 8 \quad} + \underline{\quad 2 \quad} = \underline{\quad 10 \quad}$

$\underline{\quad 10 \quad} + \underline{\quad 1 \quad} = \underline{\quad 11 \quad}$

7. $5 + 9 = \underline{\qquad}$

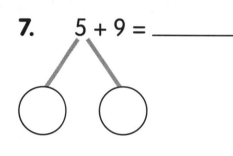

$\underline{\qquad} + \underline{\qquad} = \underline{\qquad}$

$\underline{\qquad} + \underline{\qquad} = \underline{\qquad}$

8. $6 + 6 = \underline{\qquad}$

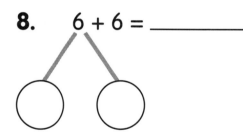

$\underline{\qquad} + \underline{\qquad} = \underline{\qquad}$

$\underline{\qquad} + \underline{\qquad} = \underline{\qquad}$

9. $7 + 8 = \underline{\qquad}$

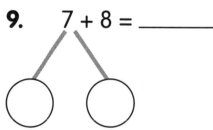

$\underline{\qquad} + \underline{\qquad} = \underline{\qquad}$

$\underline{\qquad} + \underline{\qquad} = \underline{\qquad}$

10. $9 + 9 = \underline{\qquad}$

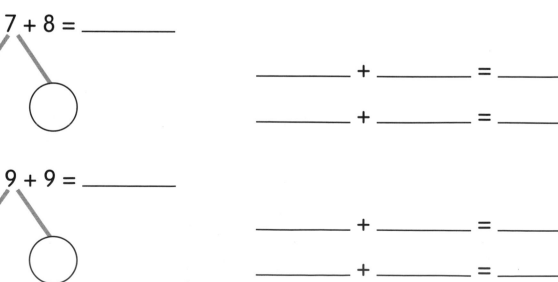

$\underline{\qquad} + \underline{\qquad} = \underline{\qquad}$

$\underline{\qquad} + \underline{\qquad} = \underline{\qquad}$

Practice 2   Ways to Add

Group the numbers into a 10 and ones.
Then add.

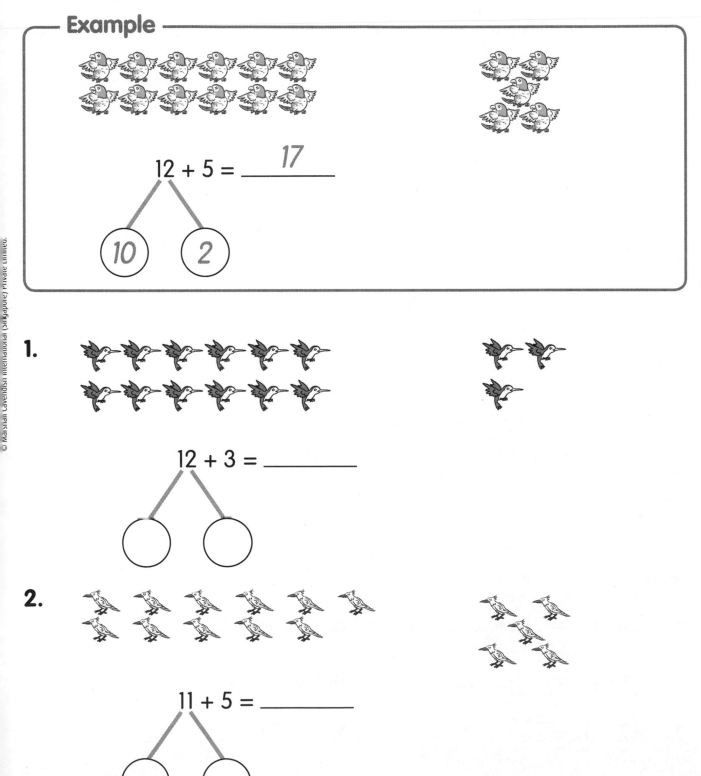

Example

12 + 5 = _____17_____

(10)   (2)

1.

12 + 3 = _____

◯   ◯

2.

11 + 5 = _____

◯   ◯

3.

$14 + 3 =$ _____

4.

$8 + 11 =$ _____

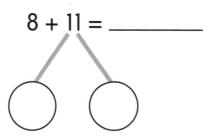

Add.

5. $15 + 2 =$ _____

6. $12 + 4 =$ _____

7. $13 + 5 =$ _____

8. $6 + 11 =$ _____

9. $7 + 12 =$ _____

10. $7 + 11 =$ _____

Practice 3   Ways to Add

Complete each addition sentence.

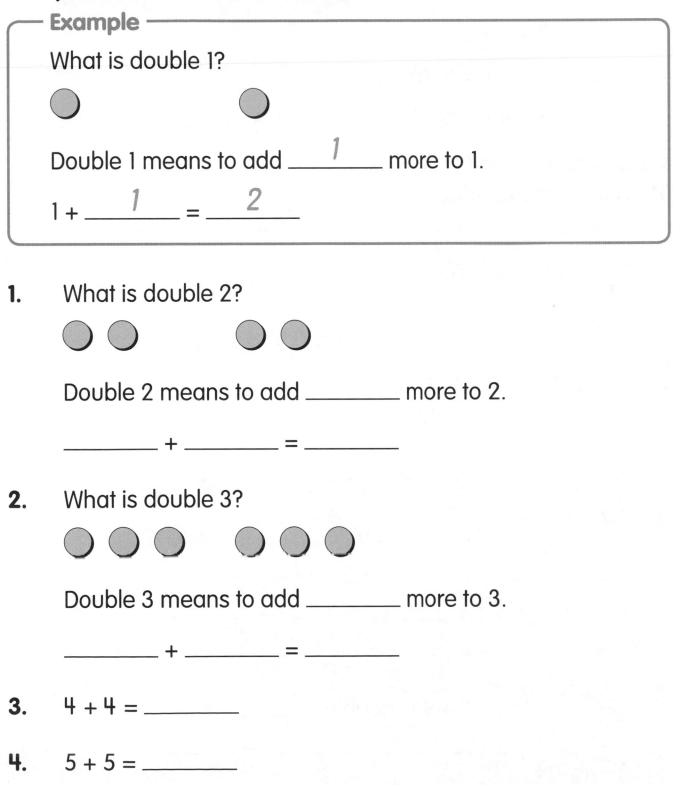

Example

What is double 1?

Double 1 means to add ____*1*____ more to 1.

1 + ____*1*____ = ____*2*____

1.   What is double 2?

Double 2 means to add _____ more to 2.

_____ + _____ = _____

2.   What is double 3?

Double 3 means to add _____ more to 3.

_____ + _____ = _____

3. $4 + 4 =$ _____

4. $5 + 5 =$ _____

Complete each addition sentence.

5.   **a.**   3 + 3 = _____

                 3 + 4 = _____

   b.   3 + 3 is double _____.

                 3 + 4 is double _____ plus _____.

Complete the number bonds.
Then fill in the blanks.

— Example —

6 + 7 = ?

⑥   ①

6 + 7 is double 6 plus ____*1*____.

6 + 6 + ____*1*____

= 12 + ____*1*____

= 13

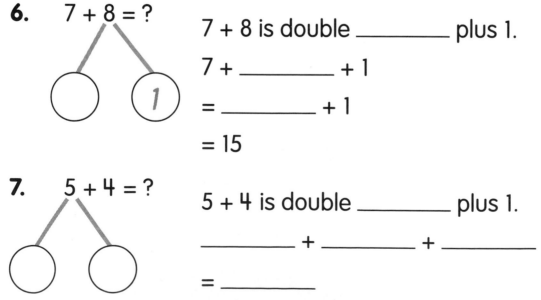

6.   7 + 8 = ?

     ◯   ①

7 + 8 is double _____ plus 1.

7 + _____ + 1

= _____ + 1

= 15

7.   5 + 4 = ?

     ◯   ◯

5 + 4 is double _____ plus 1.

_____ + _____ + _____

= _____

Use doubles facts to complete the addition sentences.

Example

$\boxed{2} + \boxed{2} = 4$

8. $\boxed{} + \boxed{} = 0$

9. $\boxed{} + \boxed{} = 12$

10. $\boxed{} + \boxed{} = 10$

11. $\boxed{} + \boxed{} = 16$

12. $\boxed{} + \boxed{} = 18$

13. $\boxed{} + \boxed{} = 20$

Add the doubles-plus one numbers.
Use doubles facts to help you.
Then write the doubles fact you used.

> **Example**
>
> $5 + 6 =$ _____11_____
>
> Doubles fact: ___5___ + ___5___ = ___10___

14. $7 + 6 =$ _____

Doubles fact: _____ + _____ = _____

15. $7 + 8 =$ _____

Doubles fact: _____ + _____ = _____

16. $9 + 10 =$ _____

Doubles fact: _____ + _____ = _____

17. $8 + 9 =$ _____

Doubles fact: _____ + _____ = _____

Practice 4 Ways to Subtract

Group the numbers into a 10 and ones.
Then subtract.

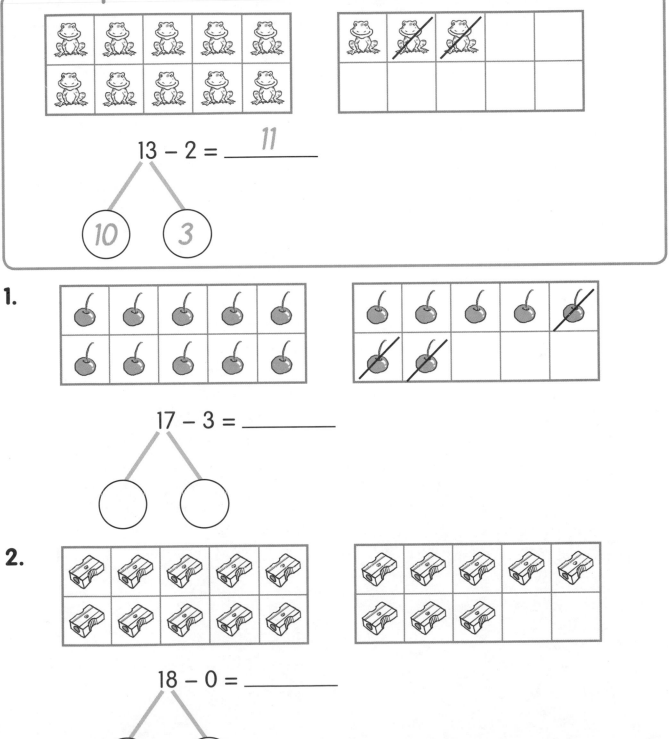

Example

$13 - 2 =$ _____ 11

10   3

1.

$17 - 3 =$ _____

2.

$18 - 0 =$ _____

3.

18 − 4 = _____

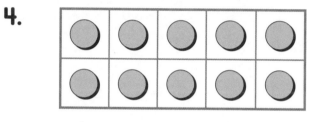

_____ − _____ = _____

_____ + _____ = _____

4.

19 − 5 = _____

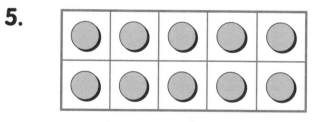

_____ − _____ = _____

_____ + _____ = _____

5.

17 − 6 = _____

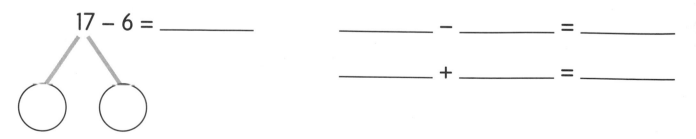

_____ − _____ = _____

_____ + _____ = _____

Group the numbers into a 10 and ones.
Then subtract.

Example

12 – 1 = ___11___

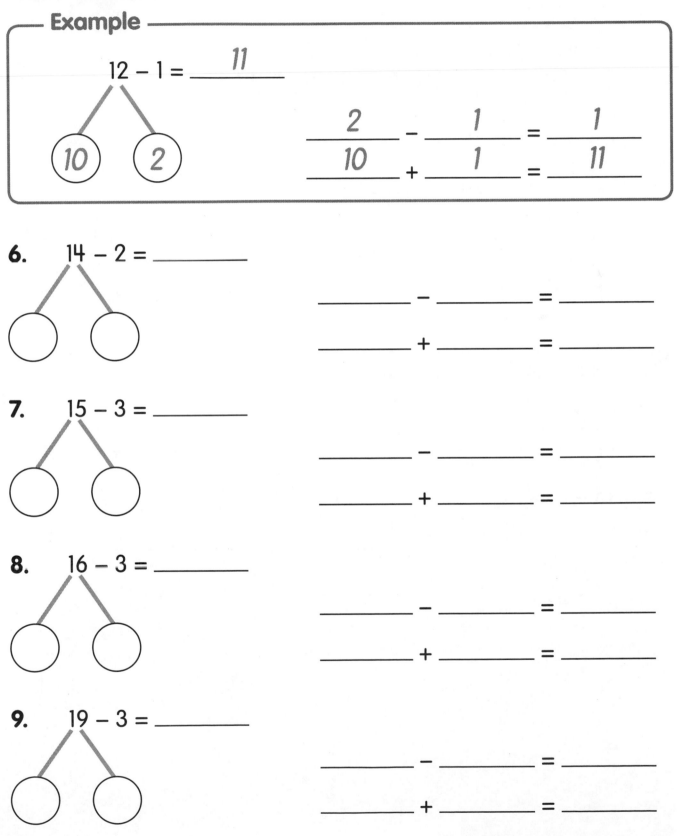

10   2

$\dfrac{2}{10} - \dfrac{1}{1} = \dfrac{1}{}$

_____ + _____ = ___11___

6.   14 – 2 = _____

○ ○

_____ – _____ = _____

_____ + _____ = _____

7.   15 – 3 = _____

○ ○

_____ – _____ = _____

_____ + _____ = _____

8.   16 – 3 = _____

○ ○

_____ – _____ = _____

_____ + _____ = _____

9.   19 – 3 = _____

○ ○

_____ – _____ = _____

_____ + _____ = _____

Group the numbers into a 10 and ones.
Then subtract.

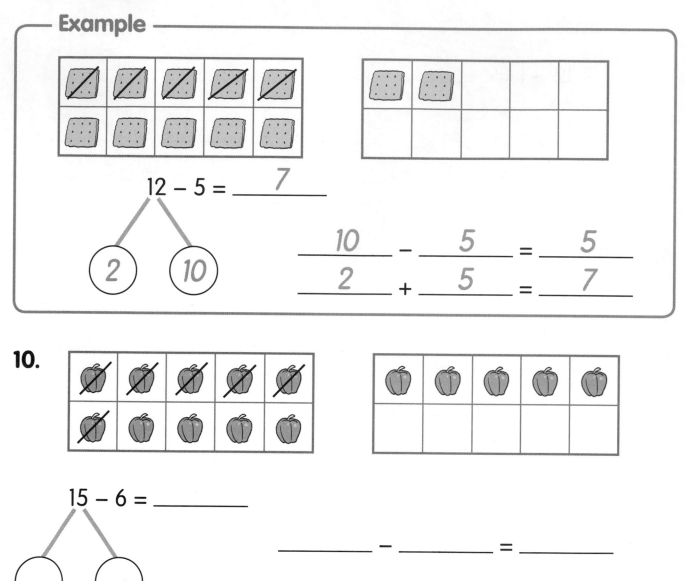

Example

$12 - 5 =$ ____7____

2   10

10 − 5 = 5
2 + 5 = 7

10.

$15 - 6 =$ _____

____ − ____ = ____

____ + ____ = ____

11.

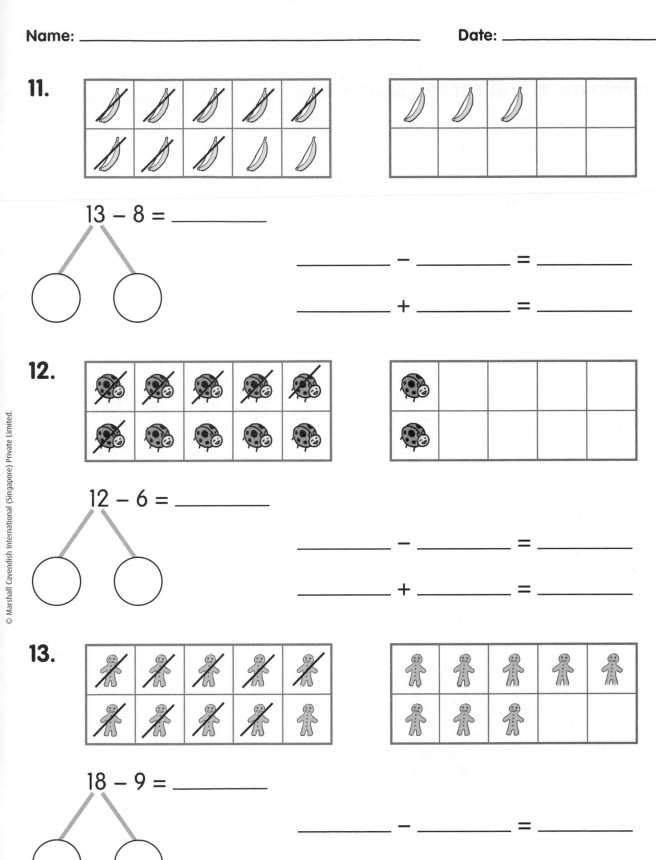

13 − 8 = _____

○   ○

_____ − _____ = _____

_____ + _____ = _____

12.

12 − 6 = _____

○   ○

_____ − _____ = _____

_____ + _____ = _____

13.

18 − 9 = _____

○   ○

_____ − _____ = _____

_____ + _____ = _____

Complete each subtraction sentence.

14.

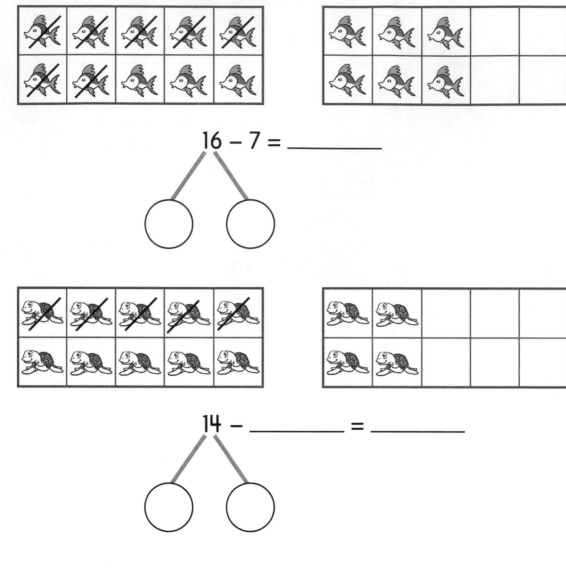

$$16 - 7 = \underline{\hspace{2cm}}$$

15.

$$14 - \underline{\hspace{2cm}} = \underline{\hspace{2cm}}$$

16.

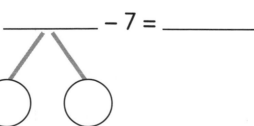

$$\underline{\hspace{2cm}} - 7 = \underline{\hspace{2cm}}$$

Complete each subtraction sentence.

17.

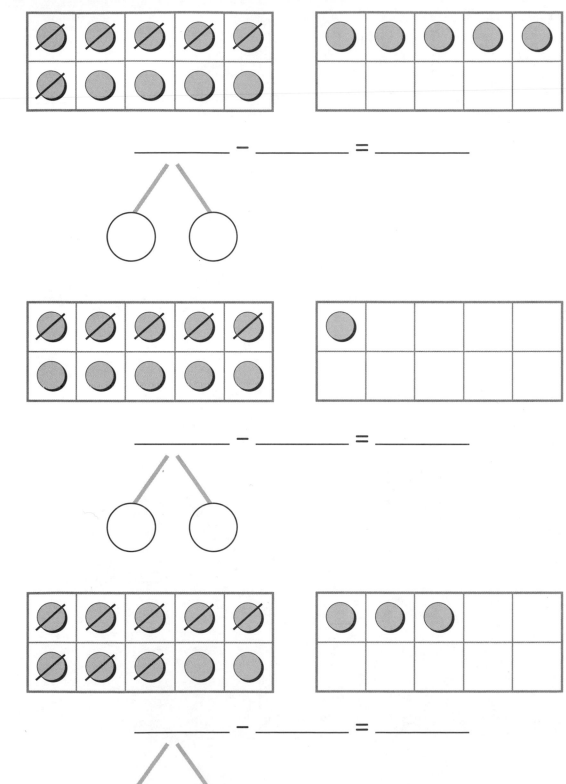

_____ − _____ = _____

18.

_____ − _____ = _____

19.

_____ − _____ = _____

Complete the number bonds.
Subtract.

20. 16 – 6 = _____

21. 14 – 7 = _____

Solve.

22. Which number fell into the number machine?
Write the number in the ◯.

Practice 5 Real-World Problems: Addition and Subtraction Facts

Solve.

1. Mandy has 5 toy bears.
She has 5 toy dogs.
How many toys does she
have in all?

Mandy has _____ toys in all.

2. 6 children are on the
merry-go-round.
6 more children join them.
How many children are
there now?

There are _____ children now.

3. Sam has 8 marbles.
Lamont gives him 9 marbles.
How many marbles does Sam
have now?

Sam has _____ marbles now.

4. Sue has 13 green ribbons and red ribbons.
5 ribbons are green.
How many red ribbons does Sue have?

Sue has _____ red ribbons.

5. Malika makes 12 bracelets.
She sells some bracelets.
She has 4 bracelets left.
How many bracelets does Malika sell?

Malika sells _____ bracelets.

6. Al makes 16 butterfly knots.
He gives 9 butterfly knots to his friends.
How many butterfly knots does Al have left?

Al has _____ butterfly knots left.

Put On Your Thinking Cap!

Challenging Practice

Write + or – in each circle.

1. 10 ◯ 6 = 4

2. 7 ◯ 5 = 12

3. 16 ◯ 9 = 7

4. 9 ◯ 7 = 16

5. 11 ◯ 3 = 14

6. 14 ◯ 6 = 20

7. 17 ◯ 2 = 15

8. 12 ◯ 8 = 20

Fill in the blanks.

9. 18 – _____ = 10

10. _____ – 9 = 11

11. 20 – _____ = 20

12. _____ – 6 = 6

13. _____ + 3 = 12

14. _____ + 5 = 13

Solve.

15. Dane gets 2 baskets in a computer game.
His total score is 16.

    a.   Color 2 baskets that he gets.

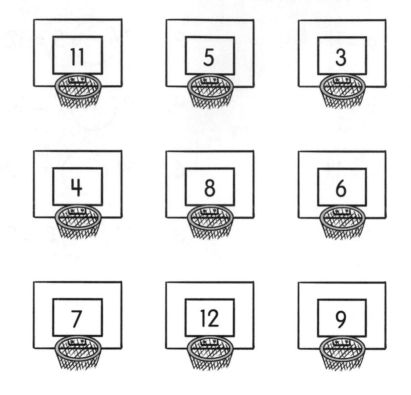

    b.   Which are the 2 baskets that he got?
Write an addition sentence for them.

        _____ + _____ = 16

    c.   Look for other answers.
Write them here.

        _____ + _____ = 16

        _____ + _____ = 16

Put On Your Thinking Cap!

Problem Solving

Solve.

Ed did 6 more cartwheels than Lila.
How many cartwheels did
Ed and Lila each do?

Write four possible pairs of numbers.
The total number of cartwheels cannot be more than 20.

1.   If Lila did _____ cartwheels, then Ed did _____ cartwheels.

2.   If Lila did _____ cartwheels, then Ed did _____ cartwheels.

3.   If Ed did _____ cartwheels, then Lila did _____ cartwheels.

4.   If Ed did _____ cartwheels, then Lila did _____ cartwheels.

Fill in each ◯ with any of these numbers.
Use each number once.

5.

| 2 | 3 | 5 | 6 |

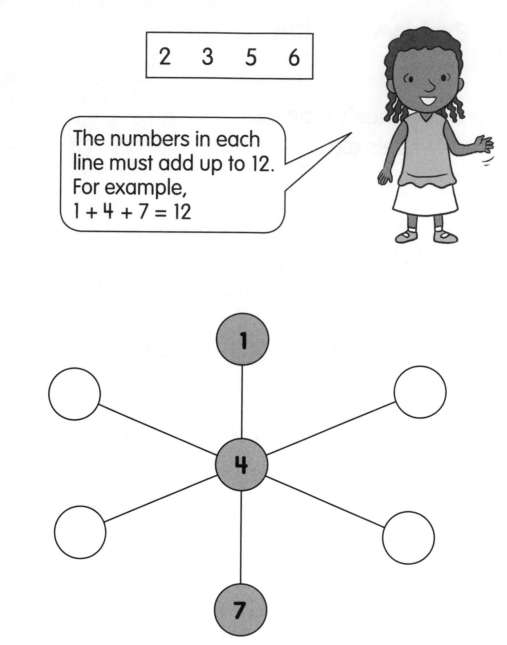

The numbers in each
line must add up to 12.
For example,
$1 + 4 + 7 = 12$

Chapter Review/Test

Vocabulary

Circle the correct answers.

1.   Which numbers are the <u>same</u>?

   4   9   6   0   4

2.   Which fact is a doubles fact?

   9 + 1 = 10   4 + 8 = 12   9 + 9 = 18

3.   Which fact is a doubles plus one fact?

   1 + 2 = 3   3 + 3 = 6   9 + 2 = 11

Concepts and Skills

Fill in the blanks.

4.   6 + 5 = _____

5.   9 + 6 = _____

Complete the number bonds.
Then fill in the blanks.

6.   15 + 4 = _____

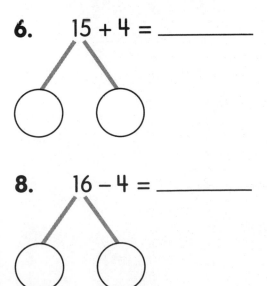

7.   6 + 14 = _____

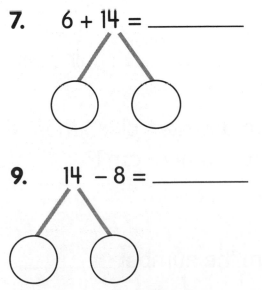

8.   16 − 4 = _____

9.   14 − 8 = _____

Fill in the blanks.

10.   11 + 9 = _____

11.   12 − 5 = _____

Problem Solving

Solve.

12.   Andy has 9 stickers.
His sister gives him 5 more.
How many stickers does
Andy have in all?

Andy has _____ stickers in all.

13.   Tia has 14 hair clips.
She gives 7 hair clips to her sister.
How many hair clips does Tia
have left?

Tia has _____ hair clips left.

14.   I am double 6 plus 1 more.
What number am I?

I am the number _____.

Name: _____   Date: _____

Length

Practice 1   Comparing Two Things

Circle the correct answer.

Example

Which is longer?

1.   Who is taller?

2.   Which is shorter?

Fill in the blanks.

Example

Which is longer?
Which is shorter?

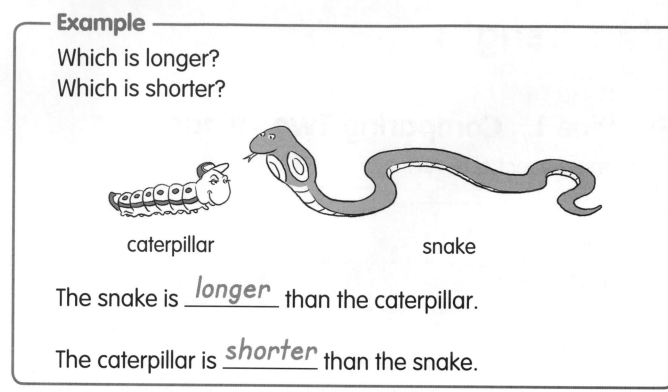

caterpillar   snake

The snake is _*longer*_ than the caterpillar.

The caterpillar is _*shorter*_ than the snake.

---

3.   Which is shorter?
Which is taller?

The giraffe is _____ than the tree.

The tree is _____ than the giraffe.

Name: _____ **Date:** _____

4. Which is longer?
Which is shorter

The train is _____ than the truck.

The truck is _____ than the train.

5. Which is shorter?
Which is taller?

swan   duck

The duck is _____ than the swan.

The swan is _____ than the duck.

Draw.

> **Example**
>
> a longer arrow
>
>

6. a shorter tree

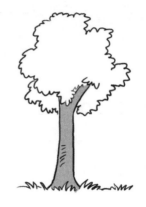

7. a longer and taller ship

Practice 2   Comparing More Than Two Things

Look at the picture.
Fill in the blanks with the correct names.

Rolo   Lad   Biff

1.   _____ is taller than Biff.

2.   Biff is taller than _____.

3.   So, Lad is also taller than _____.

Read.
Then draw the tails on the mouse and dog.

4.   The mouse's tail is longer than the cat's tail.
     The cat's tail is longer the dog's tail.
     So, the mouse's tail is longer than the dog's tail.

Color.

Example

the longest string of beads

5. the shortest vegetable

6. the girl with the longest hair

7. the tallest animal

Fill in the blanks with *taller, tallest, shorter,* or *shortest*.

ostrich   elephant   bear   giraffe

8. The giraffe is the _____ animal.

9. The ostrich is _____ than the bear.

10. The _____ animal is the bear.

11. The ostrich is _____ than the elephant.

Look at the picture.
Fill in the blanks.

very curly wire

curly wire

straight wire

12. The _____ is longer than the curly wire.

13. The curly wire is longer than the _____.

14. The _____ is the longest wire.

Math Journal

Help Jamie put his toys away. Read.
Then cut out the toys on page 233 and paste them on the shelf.

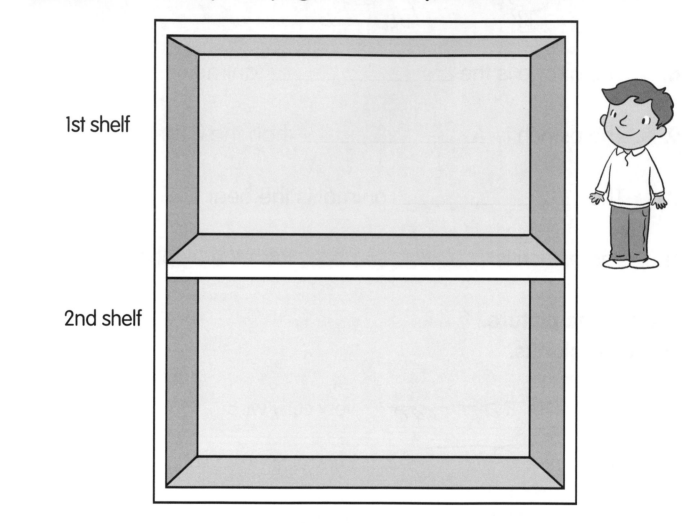

1st shelf

2nd shelf

1st shelf	• teddy bear • toy taller than the teddy bear
2nd shelf	• toy shorter than the teddy bear • longest toy • toy shorter than the toy train

© Marshall Cavendish International (Singapore) Private Limited.

Practice 3   Using A Start Line

Cut out the caterpillars.
Paste them on the box in the order shown.

1.

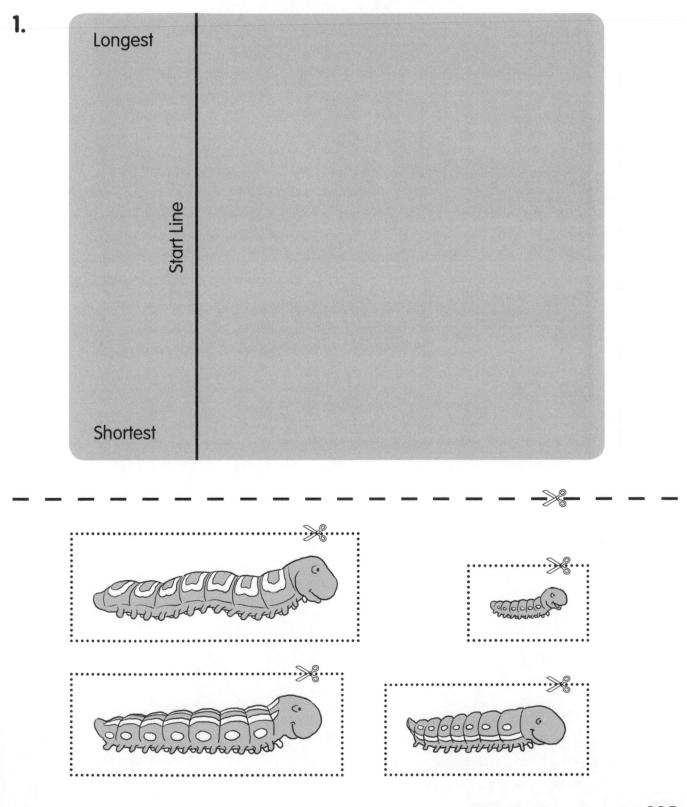

Draw 2 more pencils.
Color the longest pencil blue.
Color the shortest pencil green.

2. Start Line

Practice 4   Measuring Things

Count.
Fill in the blanks.

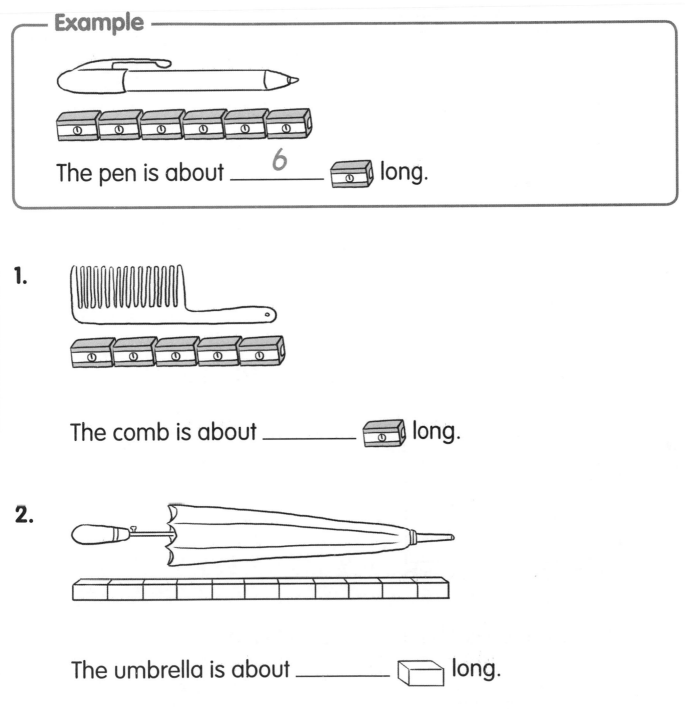

Example

The pen is about ____6____ 🟦 long.

1.

The comb is about _____ 🟦 long.

2.

The umbrella is about _____ ⬜ long.

3.

The oven is about _____ long.

4.

The photo frame is about _____ 🖇 long.

5.

The envelope is about _____ 🖇 long.

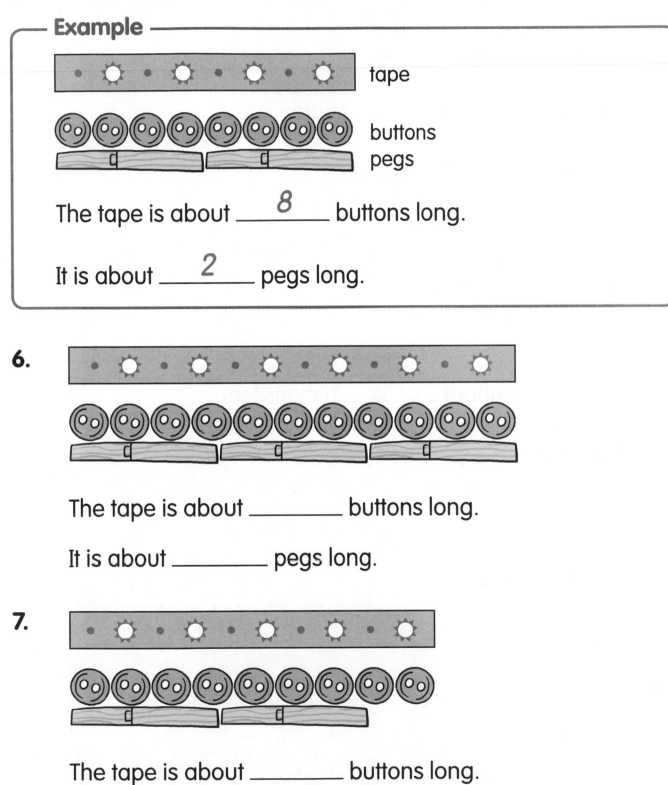

Fill in the blanks.

What is the length of each tape?

Example

tape

buttons

pegs

The tape is about ___8___ buttons long.

It is about ___2___ pegs long.

6.

The tape is about _____ buttons long.

It is about _____ pegs long.

7.

The tape is about _____ buttons long.

It is about _____ pegs long.

8.

The tape is about _____ buttons long.

It is about _____ pegs long.

9.

The tape is about _____ buttons long.

It is about _____ peg long.

Practice 5   Finding Length in Units

Count.
Fill in the blanks.

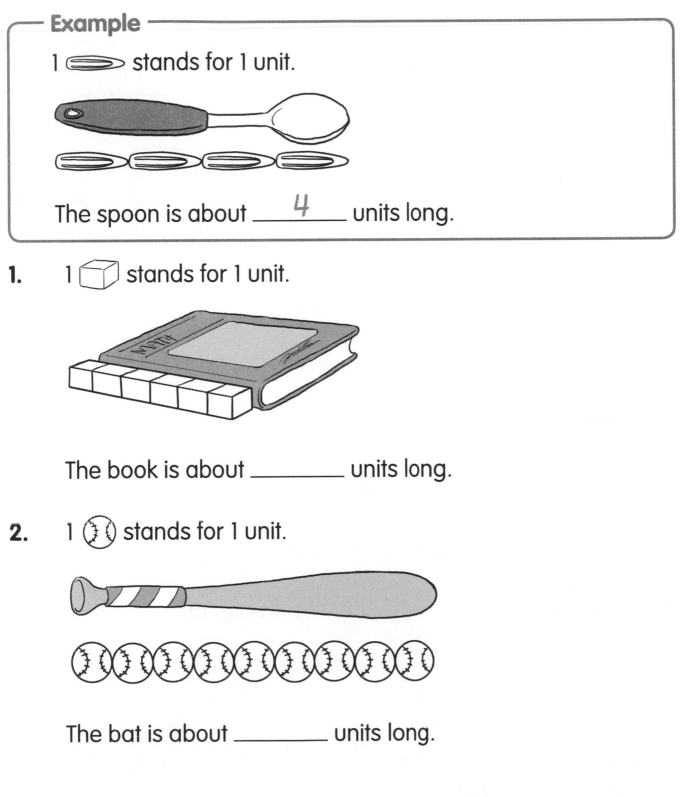

Example

1 ⬭ stands for 1 unit.

The spoon is about _____4_____ units long.

---

1.   1 ▱ stands for 1 unit.

The book is about _____ units long.

2.   1 ⚾ stands for 1 unit.

The bat is about _____ units long.

Look at the picture.
Fill in the blanks.

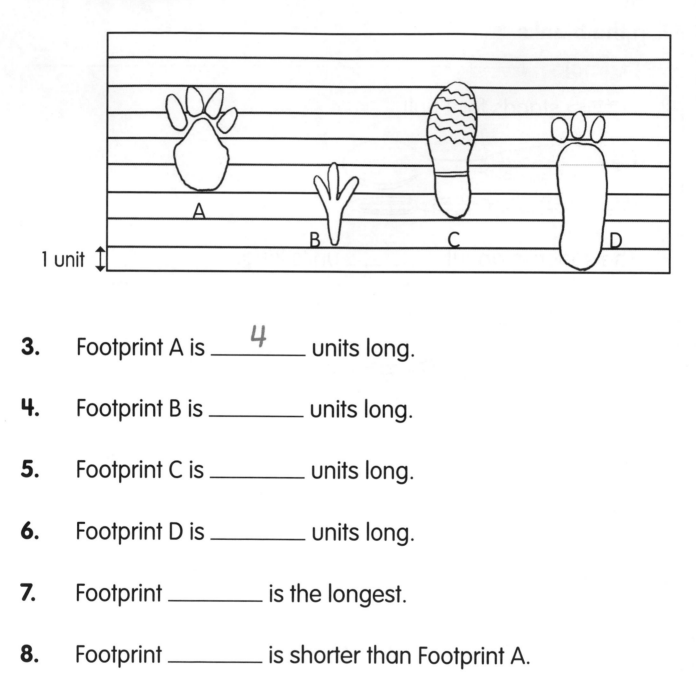

3. Footprint A is ___4___ units long.

4. Footprint B is _____ units long.

5. Footprint C is _____ units long.

6. Footprint D is _____ units long.

7. Footprint _____ is the longest.

8. Footprint _____ is shorter than Footprint A.

Look at the picture.
Fill in the blanks.

1 ☐ stands for 1 unit.

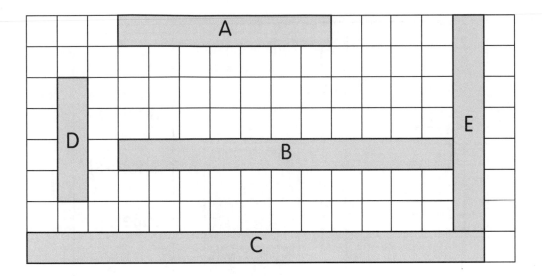

9.   Strip _____ is the longest.

It is _____ units long.

This is _____ ten and _____ ones.

10.   Strip _____ is the shortest.

It is _____ units long.

11.   Strip _____ is as long as Strip _____.

12.   Strip _____ is shorter than Strip C but longer than Strip E.

It is _____ units long.

This is _____ ten and _____ one.

Look at the picture.
Fill in the blanks. Use numbers or the words in the box.

1 ☐ stands for 1 unit.

short
shorter
shortest
taller
tallest
longer
longest

13. The table is _____ units long.

14. The bookshelf is _____ units tall.

15. Look at the stool, the table, and the bookshelf.
    The bookshelf is the _____ thing.
    The stool is _____ than the table.

16. The vase is the _____ thing in the room.

17. The string from the light is _____ than the pole
    of the fan.

Put On Your Thinking Cap!

Challenging Practice

Solve.

Mae moves the counters on a board.
The arrows show the moves.

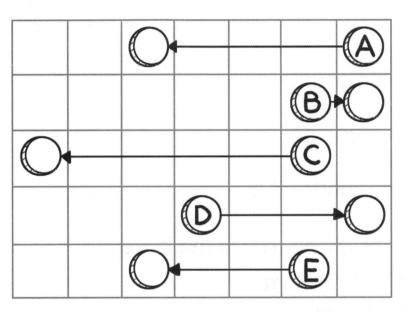

1. Which counter makes the longest move?

   _____

2. Which counter makes the shortest move?

   _____

3. Which counter moves 5 squares? _____

4. Which counters move the same length?

   _____ and _____.

Three boys are lying on a mat.

5. Who is the tallest? _____

6. Who is the shortest? _____

Write the names of the girls in the boxes.

7. Tia is taller than Nora.
Sue is the tallest.

Name: _____ **Date:** _____

Look at the picture and read.
Then draw.

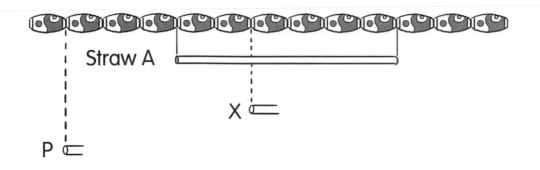

◒ stands for 1 unit.

8. Draw a straw as long as Straw A.
Start at P.

9. Draw a straw longer than Straw A.
Start at X.

Arrange the bears in order.
Write the letter.

10.

_____   _____   _____   _____
tallest

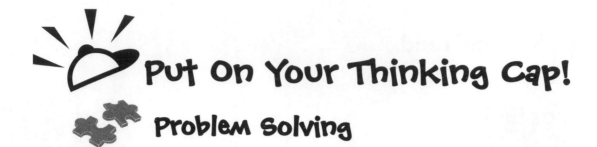

Put On Your Thinking Cap!

Problem Solving

Fill in the blanks.

1.   Tim, Ella, Rosa, and Ling knit some scarves.
     Who does each scarf belong to?

Scarf A _____

Scarf B _____

Scarf C _____

Scarf D _____

Ella's scarf is longer than Ling's scarf.

Rosa's scarf is the longest.

Ling's scarf is longer than Tim's scarf.

Name: _____   **Date:** _____

Chapter Review/Test

Vocabulary

Match.

1.   short •

tall •

short •

long •

Write _longest_ or _shortest_.

2.   pencil

ruler

paper clip

The paper clip is the _____.

The ruler is the _____.

Concepts and Skills

Draw a start line.
Read and color.

3.   Color the longest ribbon yellow.
       Color the shortest ribbon blue.

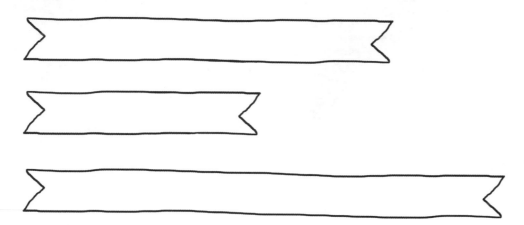

Fill in the blanks.

4.

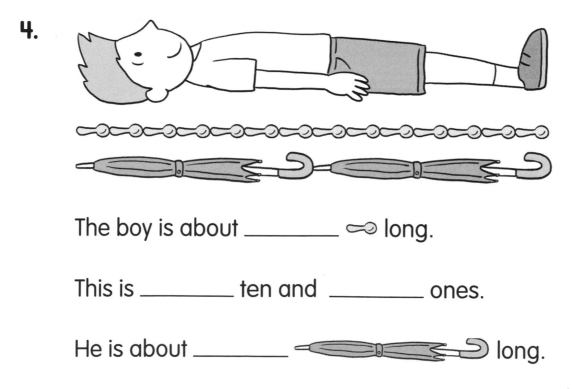

The boy is about _____ ∞ long.

This is _____ ten and _____ ones.

He is about _____ ⟨umbrella⟩ long.

Name: _____ **Date:** _____

Problem Solving

Solve.

1 ☐ stands for 1 unit.

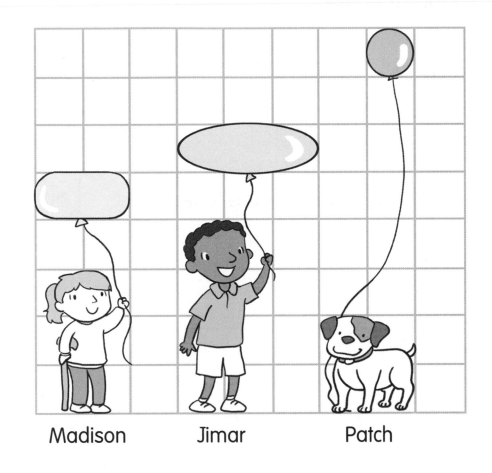

Madison   Jimar   Patch

5. Madison is _____ units tall.

6. Patch is _____ units tall and _____ units long.

7. The longest balloon is _____ units long.

8. Whose balloon has the longest string? _____

Solve.

9.   Three children are on stage.
      Ben is taller than Ally.
      Charlie is shorter than Ben.
      Ally is the shortest.

      Who is the tallest?

      _____ is the tallest.

      Who is not the shortest and not the tallest?

      _____

You may draw a picture to help you

Cumulative Review

for Chapters 7 to 9

Concepts and Skills

Circle the ten.
Then fill in the blanks.

1.

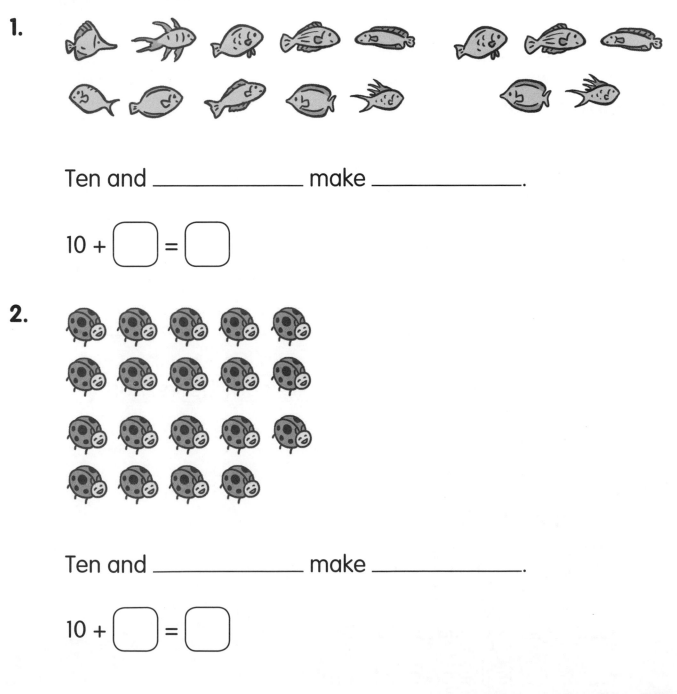

Ten and _____ make _____.

10 + ⬚ = ⬚

2.

Ten and _____ make _____.

10 + ⬚ = ⬚

Show the number.

Draw ▯ **for tens and** ▢ **for ones.**

3.

Tens	Ones

10

4.

Tens	Ones

18

Write the number.
Then fill in the blanks.

5.

Set A: _____

Set B: _____

Set _____ has _____ more teddy bears than

Set _____.

Compare.
Fill in the blanks.

6.

16	19	11	17

_____ is the least number.

_____ is the greatest number.

Name: _____   Date: _____

Complete each number pattern.

7.   9, 10, _____, 12, 13, _____, 15

8.   20, _____, 18, 17, _____, _____, 14, 13

Order the numbers from least to greatest.

9.

| 12 | 17 | 16 | 8 | 11 |

_____ _____ _____ _____ _____

Make a 10.
Then add.

10.   9 + 8 = _____   9 + _____ = 10

10 + _____ = _____

Group into a 10 and ones.
Then solve.

11.   7 + 13 = _____   **12.**   15 − 8 = _____

Complete.

13.   7 + 7 = _____   **14.**   7 + 8 = _____

15.   16 − 8 = _____   **16.**   12 − _____ = 6

Fill in the blanks.
Use the words in the box.

| shorter | shortest | longer | longest | taller | tallest |

17. Rosa is _____ than Lauren.

18. Lauren is _____ than Rosa.

19. Trey is _____ than Rosa and Lauren.

So, Trey is the _____.

20. The tail on the white dog is _____ than the tail on the spotted dog.

21. The tail on the black dog is _____ than the tail on the white dog.

22. The tail on the spotted dog is the _____.

Complete.

23. Draw a start line.
Then draw a strip that is longer than A and shorter than B.

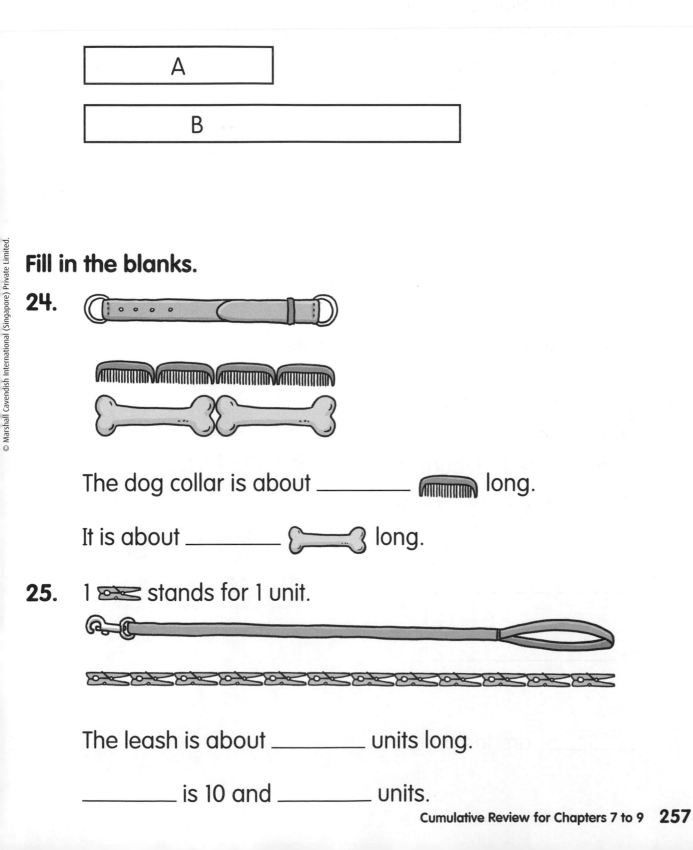

A

B

Fill in the blanks.

24.

The dog collar is about _____ 🪮 long.

It is about _____ 🦴 long.

25. 1 🧷 stands for 1 unit.

The leash is about _____ units long.

_____ is 10 and _____ units.

Problem Solving

Solve.

26. Grandma bakes 20 muffins.
She gives 8 muffins to Emily.
How many muffins does
Grandma have left?

Grandma has _____ muffins left.

27. 17 insects are in the garden.
9 are bees.
The rest are ladybugs.
How many are ladybugs?

_____ are ladybugs.

Name: _____   Date: _____

Mid-Year Review

Test Prep

Multiple Choice

Fill in the circle next to the correct answer.

1. How many stars are there?

   Ⓐ 10   Ⓑ 8   Ⓒ 7   Ⓓ 6

2. Which number is greater than 8?

   Ⓐ 8   Ⓑ 10   Ⓒ 7   Ⓓ 0

3. Which star makes 10?

   $6 + 4$ $7 + 2$ $5 + 3$ $0 + 1$

   Ⓐ   Ⓑ   Ⓒ   Ⓓ

4. Which star makes 1 less than 7?

    8 – 2   7 – 2   9 – 5   10 – 8

    Ⓐ   Ⓑ   Ⓒ   Ⓓ

5. Find the missing number.

$$\boxed{} + 9 = 10$$

Ⓐ 11   Ⓑ 8   Ⓒ 1   Ⓓ 0

6. Find the missing number.

$$8 - \boxed{} = 4$$

Ⓐ 8   Ⓑ 5   Ⓒ 4   Ⓓ 2

7. How many sides does a ◺ have?

Ⓐ 4   Ⓑ 3   Ⓒ 2   Ⓓ 0

8. How many corners does a ◯ have?

Ⓐ 0   Ⓑ 1   Ⓒ 2   Ⓓ 5

9. How are these shapes sorted?

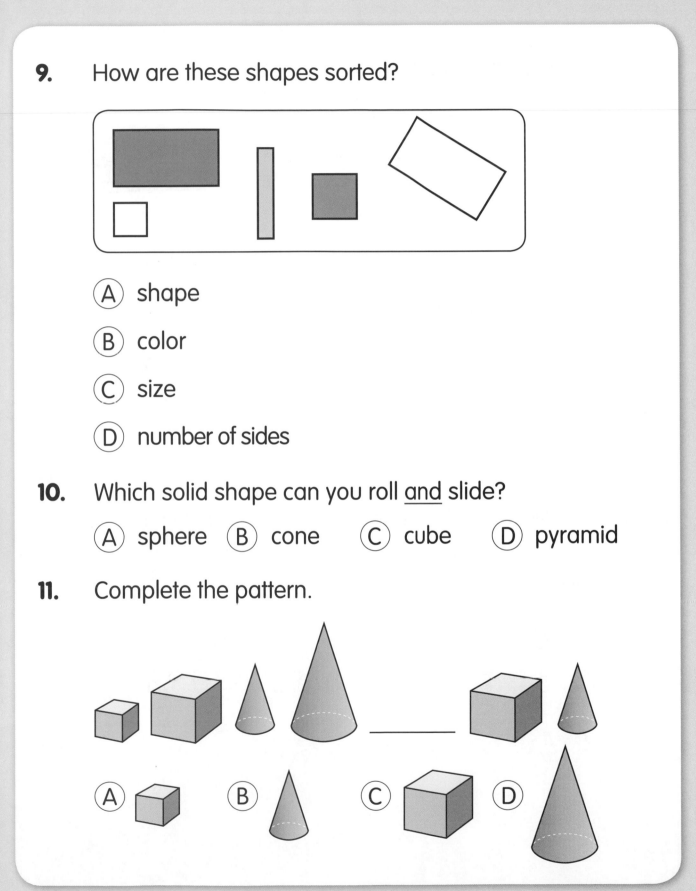

(A) shape

(B) color

(C) size

(D) number of sides

10. Which solid shape can you roll <u>and</u> slide?

(A) sphere   (B) cone   (C) cube   (D) pyramid

11. Complete the pattern.

12. In which position is the black bird?

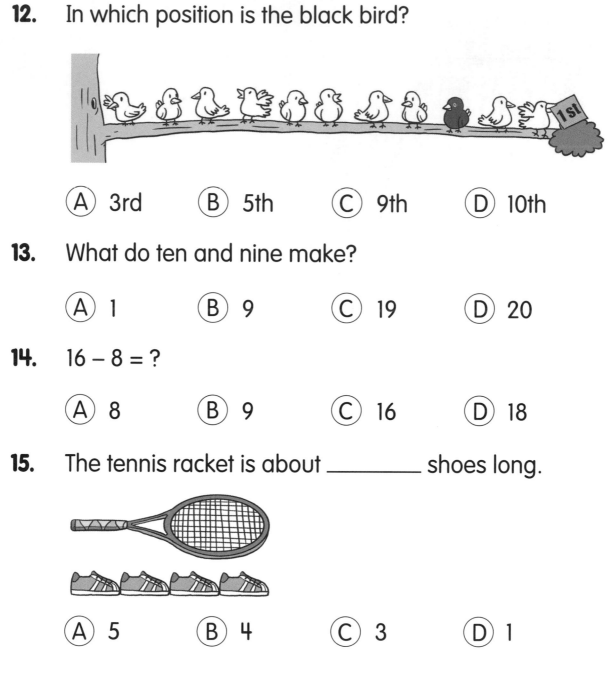

   Ⓐ 3rd   Ⓑ 5th   Ⓒ 9th   Ⓓ 10th

13. What do ten and nine make?

   Ⓐ 1   Ⓑ 9   Ⓒ 19   Ⓓ 20

14. $16 - 8 = ?$

   Ⓐ 8   Ⓑ 9   Ⓒ 16   Ⓓ 18

15. The tennis racket is about _____ shoes long.

   Ⓐ 5   Ⓑ 4   Ⓒ 3   Ⓓ 1

© Marshall Cavendish International (Singapore) Private Limited.

Short Answer

Read the questions carefully.
Write your answers in the space given.

Write the numbers in words.

16.　8　_____

17.　19　_____

18.　12　_____

Complete the number patterns.

19.　_____ 1, 2, 3, _____, 5

20.　_____, 16, 14, _____, 10, 8 _____

Add.

21.　7 + 8 = _____

22.　20 – 7 = _____

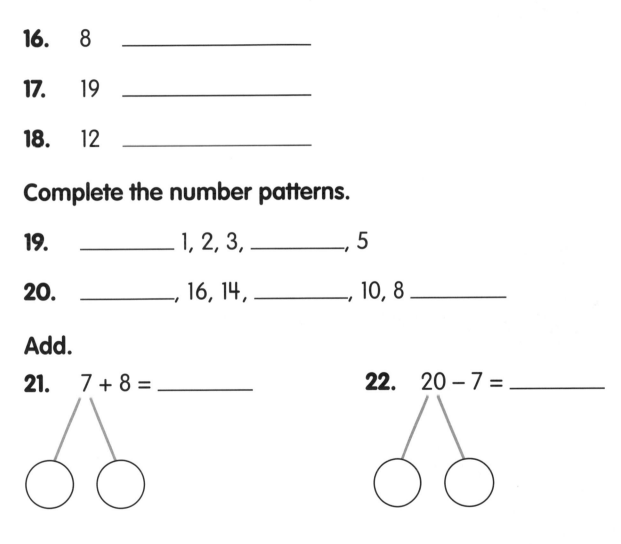

Order the numbers from greatest to least.

23.

| 19 | 9 | 20 | 10 |

_____ _____ _____ _____

Look at the picture.
Circle the words for the shapes you see.

24.

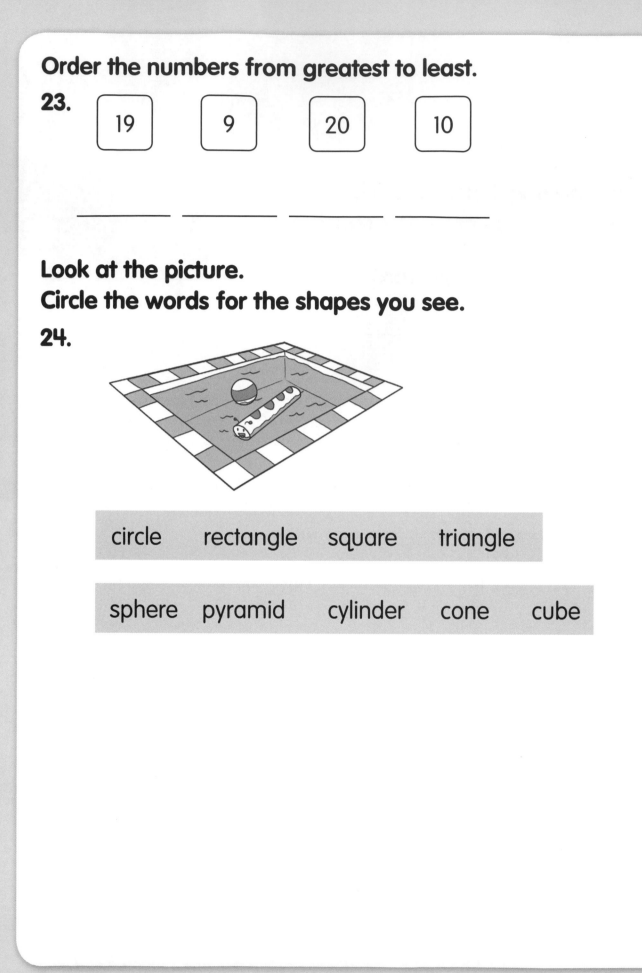

circle   rectangle   square   triangle

sphere   pyramid   cylinder   cone   cube

Name: _____   **Date:** _____

Look at the picture.
Then fill in the blanks.
Use the words in the box.

Maria Josh Liping Jamal

left	right
between	above
below	next to
first	second
third	fourth

25. Maria is last from the _____.

26. Jamal is _____ on the right.

27. Liping is _____ Josh and Jamal.

28. The mouse is _____ Josh.

Look at the picture.
Then fill in the blanks.

29. Building A is _____ units tall.

30. Building B is _____ units tall.

31. Building C is _____ units tall.

32. Building _____ is the tallest.

‡ 1 unit

A   B   C

Extended Response

Solve.

33.

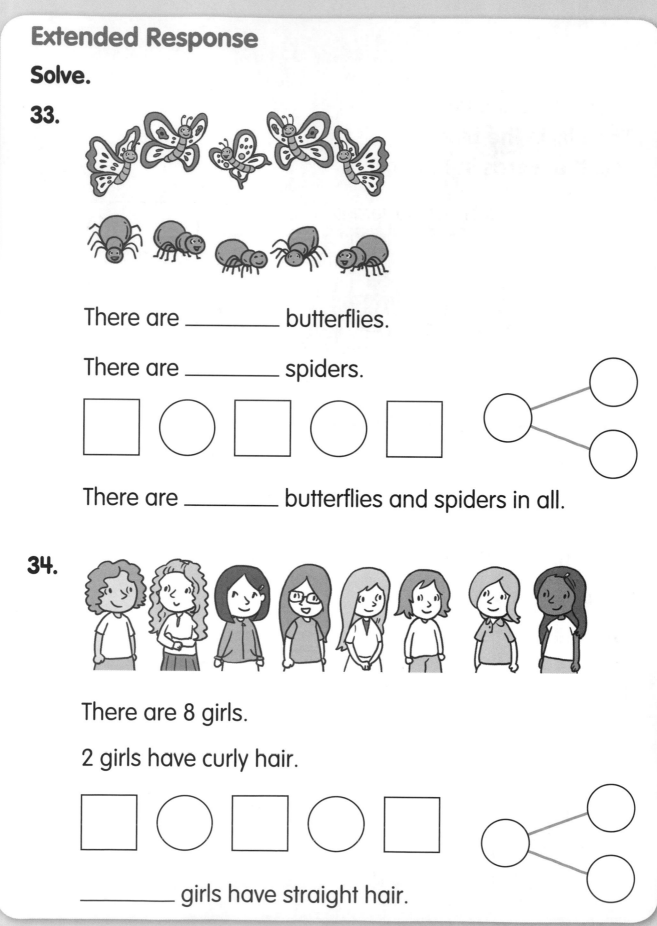

There are _____ butterflies.

There are _____ spiders.

There are _____ butterflies and spiders in all.

34.

There are 8 girls.

2 girls have curly hair.

_____ girls have straight hair.

Show the number.

Draw ▯ for tens and □ for ones.

Then fill in the blanks.

35.

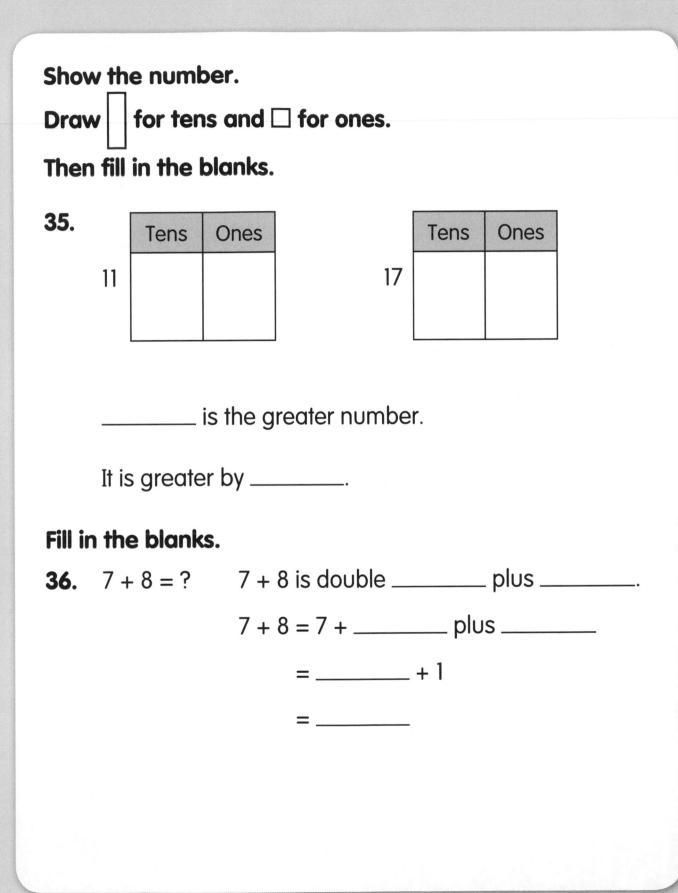

11

Tens	Ones

17

Tens	Ones

_____ is the greater number.

It is greater by _____.

Fill in the blanks.

36. 7 + 8 = ?   7 + 8 is double _____ plus _____.

7 + 8 = 7 + _____ plus _____

= _____ + 1

= _____

37. Mom has 13 buttons.
She uses some to sew a dress.
7 buttons are left.
How many buttons does Mom use?

Mom uses _____ buttons.

38. Andrew gives away 9 muffins.
He has 8 muffins left.
How many muffins did he
have at first?

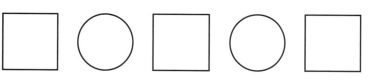

Andrew had _____ muffins at first.

39. Follow the directions:

First, draw a start line.

Next, draw a shorter arrow.

Then, draw an arrow that is longer than the other arrows.

Last, circle the shortest arrow.